ET CETERA

ET CETERA

AN ILLUSTRATED GUIDE
TO LATIN PHRASES

MAIA LEE-CHIN

ILLUSTRATIONS BY MARTA BERTELLO

Andrews McMeel
PUBLISHING®

Andrews McMeel Publishing
a division of Andrews McMeel Universal
1130 Walnut Street, Kansas City, Missouri 64106

www.andrewsmcmeel.com

24 25 26 27 28 TEN 10 9 8 7 6 5 4 3 2 1

ISBN: 978-1-5248-8634-9

Library of Congress Control Number: 2024931656

Editor: Melissa Rhodes Zahorsky
Art Director/Designer: Diane Marsh
Production Editor: Brianna Westervelt
Production Manager: Tamara Haus

ATTENTION: SCHOOLS AND BUSINESSES
Andrews McMeel books are available at quantity discounts with
bulk purchase for educational, business, or sales promotional use.
For information, please e-mail the Andrews McMeel Publishing
Special Sales Department: sales@amuniversal.com.

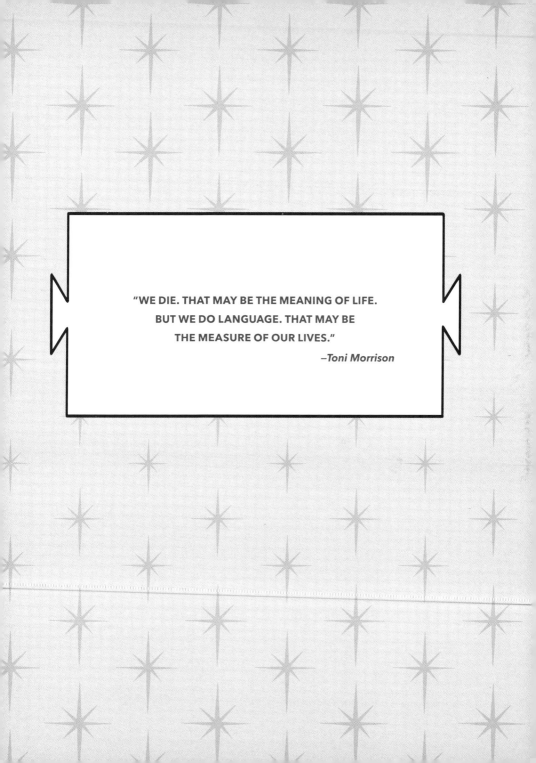

"WE DIE. THAT MAY BE THE MEANING OF LIFE.
BUT WE DO LANGUAGE. THAT MAY BE
THE MEASURE OF OUR LIVES."

—Toni Morrison

CONTENTS

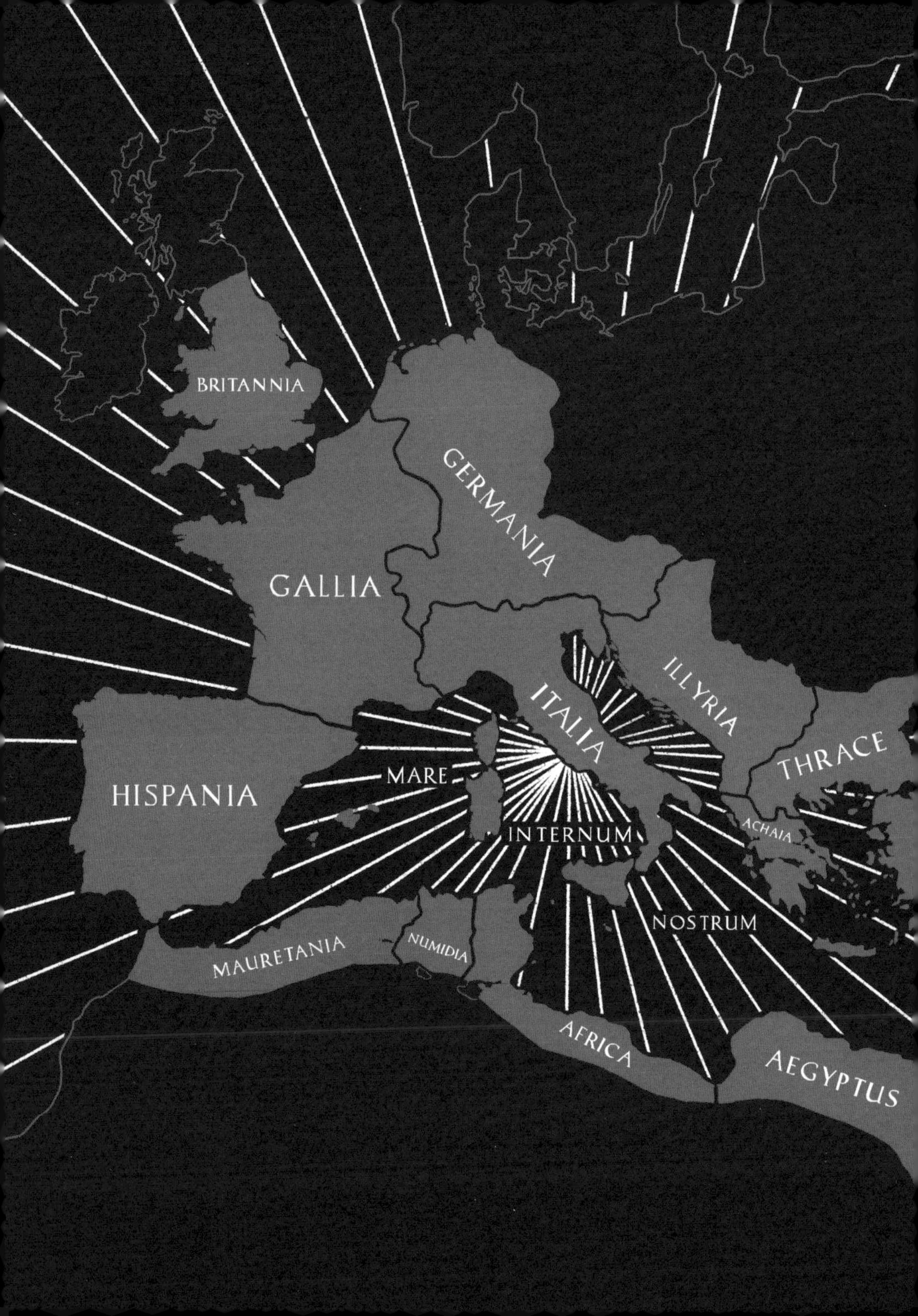
BRITANNIA
GERMANIA
GALLIA
ILLYRIA
ITALIA
THRACE
HISPANIA
MARE
INTERNUM
ACHAIA
NOSTRUM
MAURETANIA
NUMIDIA
AFRICA
AEGYPTUS

The Roman Empire

117 CE

ANATOLIA

ARMENIA

SYRIA

ASSYRIA

MESOPOTAMIA

JUDAEA

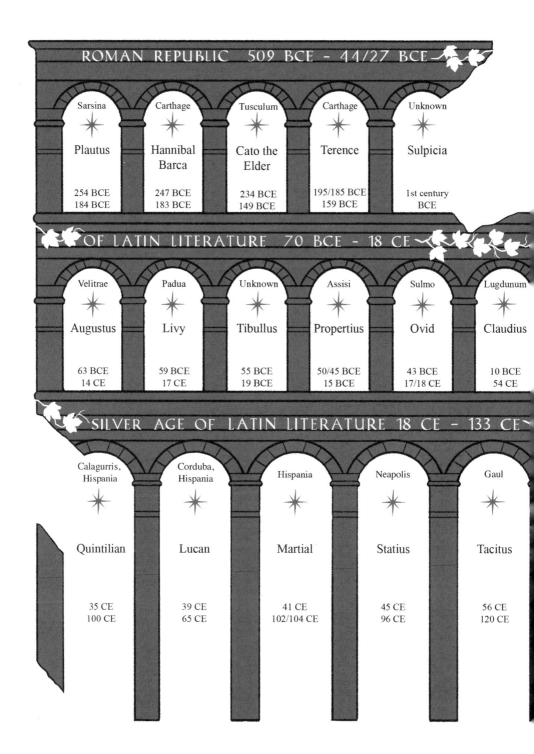

ROMAN REPUBLIC 509 BCE - 44/27 BCE

Sarsina	Carthage	Tusculum	Carthage	Unknown
Plautus	Hannibal Barca	Cato the Elder	Terence	Sulpicia
254 BCE 184 BCE	247 BCE 183 BCE	234 BCE 149 BCE	195/185 BCE 159 BCE	1st century BCE

OF LATIN LITERATURE 70 BCE - 18 CE

Velitrae	Padua	Unknown	Assisi	Sulmo	Lugdunum
Augustus	Livy	Tibullus	Propertius	Ovid	Claudius
63 BCE 14 CE	59 BCE 17 CE	55 BCE 19 BCE	50/45 BCE 15 BCE	43 BCE 17/18 CE	10 BCE 54 CE

SILVER AGE OF LATIN LITERATURE 18 CE - 133 CE

Calagurris, Hispania	Corduba, Hispania	Hispania	Neapolis	Gaul
Quintilian	Lucan	Martial	Statius	Tacitus
35 CE 100 CE	39 CE 65 CE	41 CE 102/104 CE	45 CE 96 CE	56 CE 120 CE

GOLDEN AGE

Arpinum
Cicero
106 BCE
43 BCE

Suburra, Rome
Caesar
100 BCE
44 BCE

Verona
Catullus
84 BCE
54 BCE

Mantua
Vergil
70 BCE
19 BCE

Venusia
Horace
65 BCE
8 BCE

Corduba
Seneca the Younger
4 BCE
65 CE

Antium
Caligula
12 CE
41 CE

Como
Pliny the Elder
23 CE
79 CE

Unknown
Petronius
27 CE
66 CE

Como
Pliny the Younger
61 CE
113 CE

Aquinum
Juvenal
1st century CE
2nd century CE

Syria
Manilius
1st century CE

Vindolanda
Claudia Severa
97/105 CE
unknown

Netherlands
Erasmus
1466 CE
1536 CE

INTRODUCTION

My love for the ancient Romans developed slowly. The stories never affected me as a child; Roman mythology did not capture my interest. In high school, I was forced to enroll in Latin. I considered dropping the course several times, especially while translating Julius Caesar's *De Bello Gallico*; I couldn't understand his long-winded explanations of wartime strategies, and I had no love for Roman history. But something changed when I first translated the *Aeneid* from Latin to English. Maybe because I didn't expect it, I was struck by the kinship I felt with Aeneas. His experiences were unfamiliar, yet I sensed I knew him intimately, like a dear friend. Vergil's poetry conveyed emotions I could not have expressed in my native English, but touched on themes I knew well—displacement and exodus, a responsibility to one's family, the difficulties of starting over. Aeneas founded a new life in an unfamiliar place, a responsibility known to many children of immigrants. He cared for a war-weathered people, destined to establish a Roman future.

I am a Black and Chinese woman—a second-generation American—and I explore the ancient world through these lenses. On paper, anyway, I am not your typical classicist. And yet, I have found a home in Roman stories. I carry the weight of Romans' lives wherever I go. I take them with me from conversation to conversation, in each turn of phrase: Ancient women weave stories with threads in their homes while I hem my too-long pants; the rhetoricians whittle their perfectly crafted words while I parse a politician's speech. I feel the connection so profoundly that I can't help but think that Vergil wrote the *Aeneid* for me, that I am his patron, thousands of years later.

I went to the Metropolitan Museum of Art in New York City the other day and felt overwhelmed. Standing before the sculptures in the ancient Roman and Greek section, seeing my own life reflected in their polished bronze, I wept. This feeling of on-fire recognition—of communion with a people long gone—wasn't new to me, but it was the first time this history had seemed to return my gaze. I felt deeply for those lives, and they were gone. They were thousands of years removed from me, but a narrative thread connected us, pulling and tugging.

Not everyone will feel moved to tears by *Boxer at Rest*, but I hope, dear reader, that this book will invite you into previously distant histories, blending that past with your present. Perhaps, then, these narrative threads will tangle, tying our futures together.

HOW TO USE THIS BOOK

Rather than organize the phrases alphabetically, I have employed a technique called *carmen perpetuum*, a continual narrative. The poet Ovid uses this method in the *Metamorphoses*, stringing myths together so they flow narratively from one to the next. To make the most of the book's organization, I recommend reading it from front to back as some details carry over from one entry to the next. That said, it isn't necessary to read the book this way, and the index will be a helpful tool if you decide to read it out of order. Whatever your approach, I encourage you to pause frequently, exploring whatever doorways may open for you. Above all, this book is meant to invite further exploration into the ancient world. Many resources are available to those who wish to dive deeper: excellent translations of ancient texts, museum exhibits, and other media to feed your imagination.

CURATION OF PHRASES

Each of us looks at the world through a particular frame—a unique keyhole. We can barely see beyond its edges. Sometimes things can shift into focus, and sometimes it's an optical illusion. We may spend years trying to widen our view by acquiring knowledge, reading, watching, observing, listening. But there's a limit to how much we can expand.

Although I've tried to be deliberate in the diversity of phrases I've chosen, no work of nonfiction is immune to bias. Many of the phrases in this book originate from the first centuries BCE and CE. Latin texts continued to flourish well into the Middle Ages, but I tend to focus on texts produced during the Augustan era, or the "Roman Golden Age of Literature." My knowledge from those eras is privileged—directly before my own keyhole, purposefully or not.

Five themes divide the phrases:

1. **LITERATURE:** A closer look into the literary sphere in the Roman Republic and the Empire. These movers and shakers defined how we think of Rome now.

2. **LOVE, FRIENDSHIP, AND FAMILY:** An exploration of how gender roles dominated Rome, dictating not only sexuality, but also the realms of friendship, family life, and politics.

3. **MYTHOLOGY:** Discussions of the gods and their interactions with humans, how religion affected daily life, and how that intersected with literature.

4. **MILITARY AND POWER:** A look at how war culture affected not just the Romans, but the cultures they encountered and conquered. These phrases engage with ideas that may be foreign or unthinkable to the modern reader.

5. **CULTURE AND PHILOSOPHY:** A collection of common idioms, phrases, and philosophical ideas that many highly educated people would have encountered in ancient Rome.

Each theme header is accompanied by an epigraph from a modern thinker who has engaged deeply with Classics. I've mostly chosen quotes from African-Americans and women—two groups who historically have been barred from the study of this discipline. Too often ignored, these writers bring unique perspectives that are importantly different from the interpretations popularized by mainstream classicists.

THE TITLE

When I first began telling people about this project, I found myself explaining that it was a book of Latin phrases: "Oh, you know, *carpe diem, memento mori*, etc." It took me a while to hear the third Latin phrase in that list—so commonplace in English it no longer stood out as foreign. And in this case, *et cetera*, meaning "and the rest," was shorthand for the less-remembered phrases that make up most of this volume. *The rest*, I realized, was at the heart of the book—and so it became its title.

HOW DO WE GET LATIN TEXTS?

Classical Roman literature survives mainly in fragments. Although a wealth of material remains, scholars estimate that it accounts for only about 1 percent of all Roman literature ever created. Evidence of both the missing and surviving texts comes through a physical manuscript tradition and fragments from quotations and *testimonia* (third-person accounts). Often written on papyrus—an organic material that degrades and decomposes, especially in Italy's wet and humid climate—ancient texts are rarely preserved in whole form. Even those texts kept in central archives, like the Library of Alexandria, were vulnerable to destruction. Attacks on these hubs of knowledge and information could essentially wipe away the legacies of entire civilizations. The texts that reach us often do so because someone or some group found them worthy of safekeeping, and even then, their survival was largely left to chance.

Inscriptions are some of the best-preserved evidence of Roman culture and daily life. The term "inscription" commonly refers to any material source that documents history, including epitaphs on tombstones, graffiti, dedications, stamped pottery, and even coins. Material culture can be challenging to study, given the ephemeral nature of objects, but many inscriptions survive because the engraved materials—often stone and metal—were durable, or, in the case of graffiti (marks scratched or engraved on a wall), due to favorable environmental conditions.

HOW ARE THE PHRASES PRONOUNCED?

While writing this book, I debated including a pronunciation guide for each entry. I've decided not to, given that Latin no longer has native speakers. Popularly, Latin is considered a dead language; however, linguists debate whether its usage has truly disappeared. Even today, most curricula do not include spoken Latin, but some teachers believe that speaking Latin aloud helps develop reading skills. Whether Latin is "dead" or not, it's impossible to know how native speakers would have expressed themselves colloquially. The written evidence of vernacular is limited to graffiti, letters, or sometimes plays. But by examining misspellings, transliterations, and poetic meter, scholars have begun to reconstruct how Latin might have sounded in different regions and at different time periods.

A NOTE ON NAMES

For accessibility and ease of reference, I've used common Anglicized versions of some Latin names, for example: "Vergil" for Vergilius, "Horace" for Horatius, and "Terence" for Terentius. Of course, English is a much younger language than Latin, and while these names would not have been used in ancient Rome, they are often used today.

WHERE DO PEOPLE STILL LEARN LATIN?

I was fortunate to start learning Latin at my public high school and to continue my studies at College of the Holy Cross—a small liberal arts school in Massachusetts. Many colleges and universities offer degrees in Classical Studies, Classical Languages, or Classics. There are also many free online resources and communities within Classics, like LatinTutorial on YouTube, The Latin Library database, Tufts University's Perseus Digital Library online lexicon, and many, many others.

WHO LEARNS LATIN NOW?

Classics is often associated with the so-called ivory tower, and its students are typically imagined to be white, male, middle-aged, and wealthy. However, despite its elitist reputation, the discipline has been influenced in recent years by some passionate advocates for social justice and equity. Several organizations promote the study of Classics for marginalized identities: Eos, the Women's Classical Caucus, the Mountaintop Coalition, and the Multiculturalism, Race & Ethnicity in Classics Consortium. Others, like Pharos and the now-defunct feminist publication *Eidolon*, aim to quash white supremacist uses of Classics.

LITERATURE

"ART IS IMMORTAL AND WEIGHS HEAVILY ON US,
AND MUSEUMS LEAVE US AT A LOSS FOR WORDS."

—Derek Walcott

Exegi monumentum aere perennius

MEANING: I erected monuments lasting longer than bronze
ATTRIBUTION: Horace
ORIGIN: *Odes* 3.30.1

Artists of every era yearn to be remembered for their works, but perhaps none so passionately, so boldly, as the ancient Romans. In his seminal work, *The Odes*, the poet Horace boasts of his own writing, which, he imagines, will gain him his *kleos*—his immortal legacy. Hubristic as the sentiment may seem, it has proven accurate. The poets built worlds without reams of unthinkable power, instead pushing the limits of their human language. If this is how we measure immortality—through legacy—then Horace has indeed defeated death.

Many bronze statues of Roman emperors and military leaders were melted down, their metals repurposed to make weapons. But it is much harder to destroy a word, a sentence, or an idea. As Horace knew, those have the potential to last for eternity—passed down from mother to daughter, commanding general to soldier—inscribed in memory if not in stone.

CARMEN ET ERROR

MEANING: A poem and a mistake
ATTRIBUTION: Ovid
ORIGIN: *Tristia* 2.207

In his *Tristia*, or "Sorrows," the poet Ovid tells us that he was exiled from Rome on the charge of *carmen et error*: a poem and a mistake. But which poem? And what mistake could have been punishable by exile?

Scholars believe Ovid's *Ars Amatoria*, or the "Art of Love"—a guide to the seduction of women—was the offending *carmen*. Its vulgar language and advice violated the marital norms the new Roman Empire was trying to establish. After all, it was Augustus, Rome's first emperor, who exiled Ovid; his *error* may even have been adultery committed with Augustus's daughter, Julia, who was exiled around the same time. This scandal would have blighted Augustus's political record, and so he reclaimed control by banning *Ars Amatoria* and exiling Ovid, removing him from the cultural center of Roman literature. The poet was relegated to Tomis, in modern-day Romania, where most people did not even speak Latin.

Or was he? It's unclear whether Ovid was ever actually in exile. Given his notoriety, his removal would have been a significant event in the Roman literary world, but no contemporary historians mention it. Was the *Ars Amatoria* satirical? Does Ovid write autobiographically, or has he invented an authorial front?

We have only Ovid's version of events. He insisted that the *carmen* was the *Ars Amatoria*, but he was considerably more tight-lipped about his *error*. He tells us what it is not: he did not commit murder, treason, or any other crime. In fact, he claims his true mistake was witnessing a crime committed by others—one he refuses to name.

Acta est fabula, plaudite

MEANING: Clap, the story is over
ATTRIBUTION: Augustus Caesar via Suetonius
ORIGIN: *Divus Augustus* 99

According to the Roman biographer Suetonius, Augustus's last words were "clap, the story is over"—a phrase used at the end of plays to signal that the show had finished. So what grand performance had just concluded?

Born Gaius Octavius, Augustus was just nineteen years old when, on the Ides of March 44 BCE, his great uncle Julius Caesar was brutally assassinated. Caesar had no legitimate children under Roman law but named Octavian his heir. Octavian traveled to Rome, only to discover that Marc Antony, a former ally of Caesar, had already amassed significant popular support over him. Octavian knew that a political alliance with Marc Antony would be essential to maintaining stability. After defeating Caesar's assassins, Octavian and Marc Antony divvied up the Roman territories, each covertly attempting to amass more influence. Challenging Octavian's authority, Marc Antony allied himself with Egypt's queen, Cleopatra. Even so, Octavian prevailed.

Though celebrated as Rome's peace-bringer who reinstated Republican offices, Octavian was primarily concerned with establishing his own sovereignty. He dubbed himself Augustus—a name with unmistakably religious overtones, meaning venerable—and ensured that Rome's terrain bore physical markers of his greatness. His *Res Gestae*, or "Things Done," which covered his rise to power and conveniently downplayed the civil wars that preceded his takeover, was inscribed on monuments throughout the Empire. Augustus also appointed a literary minister, Maecenas, to disseminate his vision for Rome. One of Maecenas's clients, Vergil, wrote the *Aeneid*, which furthered Augustus's divine claim to power, tracing his lineage to Aeneas, the city's mythical founder.

Augustus's aggressive public relations strategy remains effective to this day; many applaud him for his patronage of Roman poets, who worked to solidify his image as a politically savvy—and not power-hungry—ruler. But do his dying words contain a wink? A subtle acknowledgement of artifice?

Cedite Romani scriptores, cedite Grai! Nescio quid maius nascitur Iliade

MEANING: Stop, Roman writers; stop, Greeks!
Something better than the *Iliad* is born.

ATTRIBUTION: Propertius

ORIGIN: *Elegies* 2.34.59-66

9

CEDITE ROMANI
SCRIPTORES,
CEDITE GRAI!
NESCIO QUID
MAIUS NASCITUR
ILIADE

The poet Propertius praises the *Aeneid*, claiming it outshined even the *Iliad*—a work that until that point had reigned supreme within the Greek and Roman canon.

Many contemporary authors were impressed by Vergil's skill and work ethic. A perfectionist, he wrote precisely one line daily, tending to each as a mother bear does her cubs' fur. This method yielded Vergil one book approximately every decade: the *Eclogues* in 37 BCE, the *Georgics* in 29 BCE, and the *Aeneid* in 19 BCE. Today, readers are more divided on the mastery of the *Aeneid*; some accuse it of "copying" the *Iliad* and *Odyssey*. More likely, Vergil meant to reference the earlier, more established works as a way of acknowledging their influence and dialoguing with them.

Scholars divide the *Aeneid* into halves: the first half, Aeneas's exodus from Troy, is considered Odyssean, while the second half resembles the *Iliad*. Although Vergil uses Homeric Greek epic conventions, he solidifies a uniquely Roman character, one concerned with *pietas*—"duty over all else"—a stark shift from the individual glory sought by Greek heroes.

The *Aeneid*, in fact, might be considered an extension of the Trojan War epic cycle, which included the *Cypria, Iliad, Aethiopis,* "Little *Iliad*," "Sack of Troy," *Nostoi, Odyssey,* and *Telegony*. While all of these poems were performed at Greek competitions and religious festivals, the *Iliad* and *Odyssey* were the most popular. They, along with Vergil's works, managed to survive through millennia, while the other Trojan War stories were eventually lost.

What's clear, and what Vergil seems to have known himself, is that the *Aeneid* shares a lineage with the *Iliad* and *Odyssey*. It may surpass those works, as Propertius claims, but it also owes them a great deal.

PIERIUS MENTI CALOR INCIDIT

MEANING: Pierian fire fell upon my mind

ATTRIBUTION: Statius

ORIGIN: *Thebaid* 1.3

Any epic poem worth its salt begins by invoking the muse. To open the *Thebaid*, which covers the civil war between Oedipus's sons for the throne of Thebes, the writer Statius does just this. Such an opening is traditional in Roman and Greek epic poetry. It is a prayer to one of the nine goddesses, the Muses, who rule over different artistic pursuits, such as comedy, tragedy, dance, and chorus.

The gods, especially the Muses and Minerva, were said to plant divine inspiration in the minds of worthy men. Sometimes, if one were lucky, they would even take control to tell a story. In epic poetry, the author typically invokes the goddess Calliope, the leader of her sisters and the Muse of epic. More recognizable invocations of the Muses—"Sing, goddess, the rage of Achilles" (Homer's *Iliad*), "Muse, remind me of the cause" (Vergil's *Aeneid*), and "Let us begin to sing, from the Heliconian Muses" (Hesiod's *Theogony*)— ask that the goddess(es) help tell the story. In these instances, the poet simply prays that a Muse will "sing," or "remind," and the goddess obliges instantaneously—the poem continues without a hitch. But when Statius states that "Pierian fire fell upon [his] mind," he indicates that the Muses inspired him to recount the Theban civil war, but he is unsure where to begin the poem. He asks for their help, not in singing or reminding, but in deciding.

Omnis ad accessus Heliconos semita trita est

MEANING: All paths to Helicon have already been walked
ATTRIBUTION: Manilius
ORIGIN: *Astronomica* 2.50

R oman authors aspired to originality. Just as modern-day graduate students race to publish their research, Roman authors also scrambled to be "first"—to express novel ideas, to break new ground.

Manilius was one such self-professed trailblazer. In the second book of his astrological epic, he references a Greek mountain sacred to the Muses: all poets, including Homer and Hesiod, Manilius implies, had already tread the path to Mount Helicon, seeking inspiration. He would forge a different path by being the first (he claimed) to write about astrology.

And yet, although he was in conversation with Lucretius, a famous Epicurean philosopher at the time, Manilius was not widely known in the ancient world. In the Middle Ages, his work was rediscovered and found some popularity, but not to the extent of poets like Homer or Vergil. Even modern astrology enthusiasts are unlikely to have heard of Manilius. Sadly for him, not all lesser-traveled paths lead to glory.

Invita Minerva

MEANING: Unwilling Minerva
ATTRIBUTION: Various authors
ORIGIN: Colloquial

The goddess Minerva featured prominently in Roman mythology. As in the stories of Arachne and Medusa, she is often seen cursing women through transformation or disfigurement. Both feared and highly revered, she was, like the Muses, invoked at the start of creative ventures—though she was perhaps less willing to lend her help. At least, that's what's implied by the popularity of the phrase *invita Minerva*, which was shouted in moments of creative frustration. Found in poetry and prose, the phrase was likely part of Romans' everyday speech.

There is an element of self-criticism to the lament; its speaker is frustrated by Minerva, but also their own lack of talent, wisdom, or experience. Though less common, the inverse phrase also existed: *non invita Minerva*, or "not unwilling Minerva." The double negative formed a positive: the goddess had lent her aid.

SATURA QUIDEM TOTA NOSTRA EST

MEANING: At least satire is entirely ours
ATTRIBUTION: Quintilian
ORIGIN: *Institutio Oratoria* 10.1.93-5

It was common for ancient literary scholars and critics to attempt to trace Roman traditions back to Greek influences. For Roman epic poets like Livius, Ennius, and Vergil, the precedent was Homer. Plautus, the Roman dramatist, looked to Diphilus; Callimachus's poetry inspired Catullus and Sulpicia; and the Roman historian Livy traced his roots to Herodotus and Thucydides. So when the first-century rhetorician Quintilian claimed, somewhat facetiously, that satire was "entirely (Rome's)," he referenced, and perhaps even poked fun at, Rome's cultural dependence upon earlier civilizations.

But the joke was on Quintilian, for even Roman satire—a genre of poetry markedly different from modern satire—was not original to Rome. One hundred years before the *Institutio Oratoria*, Horace had rather harshly pointed this out, claiming that Lucilius, the so-called father of Roman satire, had relied on Greek precedent to "create" the form.

It is perhaps natural to wish for intellectual independence, but today we understand that few innovations are truly original; most "new" technologies rely on some prior example. Nevertheless, ancient Romans are praised today for their radical transformation of the world as we know it. Satire may not have been properly "theirs," but they did give it its name.

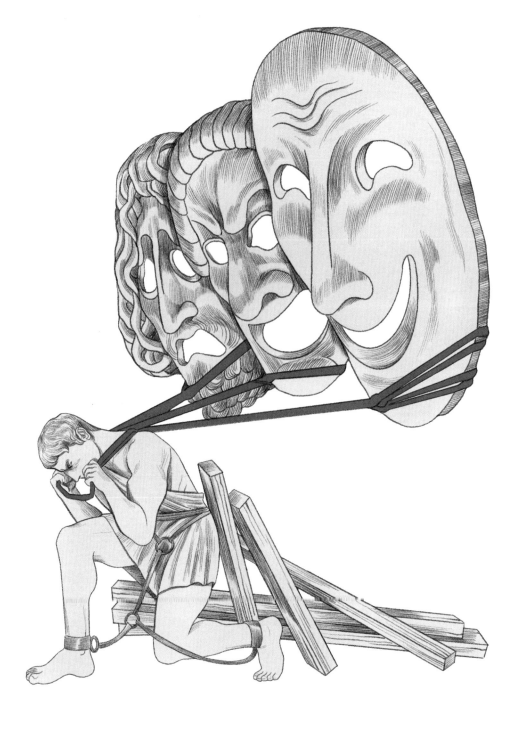

FACIAM UT MEI MEMINERIS

MEANING: I will force you to remember me
ATTRIBUTION: Plautus
ORIGIN: *Persa* 4.3.24

Persa is a play about an enslaved person who tricks a pimp into giving him enough money to procure his girlfriend's freedom. As part of an elaborate scam involving purchasing an enslaved Persian girl who is actually free, the main character, Toxilus, delivers the sales pitch of a lifetime, introducing it with this humorous, if slightly threatening, line: "I will force you to remember me."

The play is a *palliata*, a comedy written in Latin and adapted from Greek sources. With each translated line, each painfully deliberate word choice, Plautus carves a Roman cultural artifact from Greek material.

At the time, *Persa* was considered a subversive Roman play because Toxilus was not a rich man but, instead, a clever enslaved man. It was unusual to see a positive portrayal of an enslaved person, and doubly so given that most actors would have been enslaved themselves.

Theater was highly associated with slavery in Rome. Actors and dancers were classed together with sex workers, thought to be selling their bodies for the entertainment of others. In fact, if a full citizen wanted to become an actor, they forfeited certain rights, including the rights to testify in court and to vote. Although no material evidence of this remains, scholars believe actors may have worn masks to hide their identities from the audience. The masks typically represented stock characters, like the *senex iratus*—the angry old man—or the *miles gloriosus*—the braggart soldier.

Though acting was perceived as lowly, sponsoring plays delivered political gains. Public officials called *aediles* maintained public buildings and organized religious festivals, where plays like *Persa* were performed competitively. Sometimes, *aediles* even invested their own money to sponsor public projects, ironically living out Toxilus's line, asking—or rather, forcing—voters to remember them come election time.

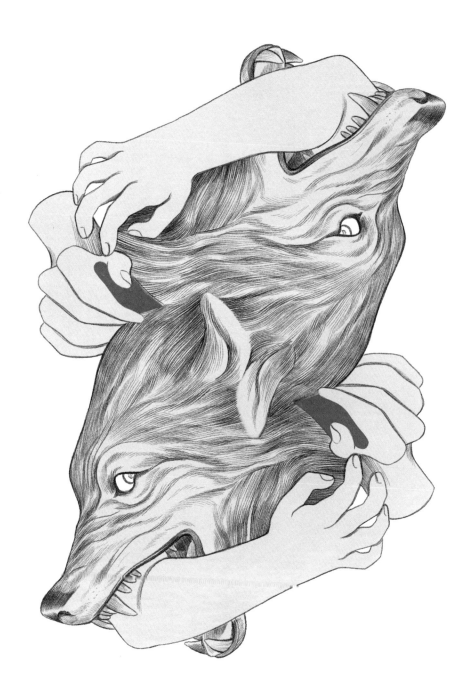

Auribus teneo lupum

MEANING: I am holding a wolf by the ears
ATTRIBUTION: Terence
ORIGIN: *Phormio* 3.2

Despite his death at the young age of twenty-five, Terence is credited as one of the foremost writers of Roman comedy. This phrase comes from his play *Phormio*, or "Parasite," in which the character Antipho, caught in a scheme and faced with a difficult choice, says, "I'm holding a wolf by the ears, and I don't know how to get rid of it nor keep holding onto it." Each of Antipho's options is potentially dangerous, yet he must choose one of the two. Thus, to "hold a wolf by the ears" is to face a problem without a clear solution, or one with two unsavory outcomes.

Terence's plays were unpopular while he was alive; however, his work reemerged with the revival of the manuscript tradition in medieval Europe. To keep them busy (and prevent them from sin), monks were tasked with copying ancient texts. Because Terence's plays used vernacular Latin and simple grammatical constructions, they made excellent copy material—and it didn't hurt that his language was plain and humorous: suitable for monks who found the work grueling.

While later evidence suggests that classical texts fell out of favor with the Catholic church, Terence's words are still referenced today. Such a phrase is evergreen, not because the imagery still makes sense in a modern context but because the experience of being caught, as it were, between a rock and a hard place, between Scylla and Charybdis, is universal.

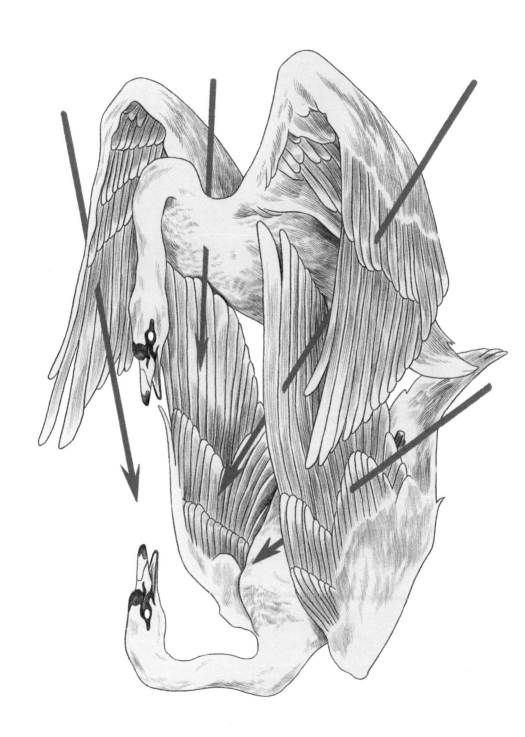

Cygnea cantio

MEANING: Swan song
ATTRIBUTION: Erasmus
ORIGIN: Roman metaphor

The medieval Dutch scholar Erasmus includes this phrase in his *Adagia*, a book of Latin and Greek proverbs, referring to the swan's dying song, which was also, according to many Roman poets, its most beautiful.

Although we find *cygnea cantio* in this form from Erasmus, the concept is an ancient one. The Roman poet Ovid describes the swan as a singer of funeral dirges: *Carmina iam moriens canit exequialia cygnus* ("The swan sings a funeral song, now dying"). The swan is clairvoyant, aware of its coming death and the lamenting ahead. Another Roman poet, Martial, claims that swans are singers of their own demise. And likewise, in Homeric poetry, such as the *Iliad*, warriors seem to herald their own deaths with a final display of excellence. This was known as an *aristeia*—a warrior's last and most impressive performance.

But swans were not exclusively associated with death and mourning in the ancient world. They were also considered positive omens. In his role as an imperial poet for Augustus, Vergil sought to reclaim the religious practice of augury—looking to birds for signs from the gods. Ancient religious practices tied Augustus to the *mos maiorum*, "the way of the ancestors," and affirmed his rightful place as a political leader. In the *Aeneid*, Venus, in disguise, interprets the escape of twelve swans from an eagle's attack as a harbinger of victory for her son, Aeneas, one of Augustus's supposed ancestors.

Today, swans remain associated with positive traits—namely, gracefulness and beauty—but, as symbols, they are not without a shadow, a sense of foreboding, the origins of which may be their "song" described by Ovid and Martial and echoed by Homer. Even so, in modern popular culture, one's "swan song" does not necessarily portend death so much as retirement; it describes the final performance or work of one's career. As with many Latin phrases still uttered today, though its meaning is essentially the same, some of the expression's original drama has been stripped away.

LOVE, FRIENDSHIP, AND FAMILY

"SO, WHO SHALL I BE? I HAVE GONE BACK AND FORTH IN VAIN
THROUGH THE AGES AND THROUGH THE STORIES WITHIN MY
REACH, YET FIND NO WOMAN INTO WHOM I CAN SLIP."

–Hélène Cixous

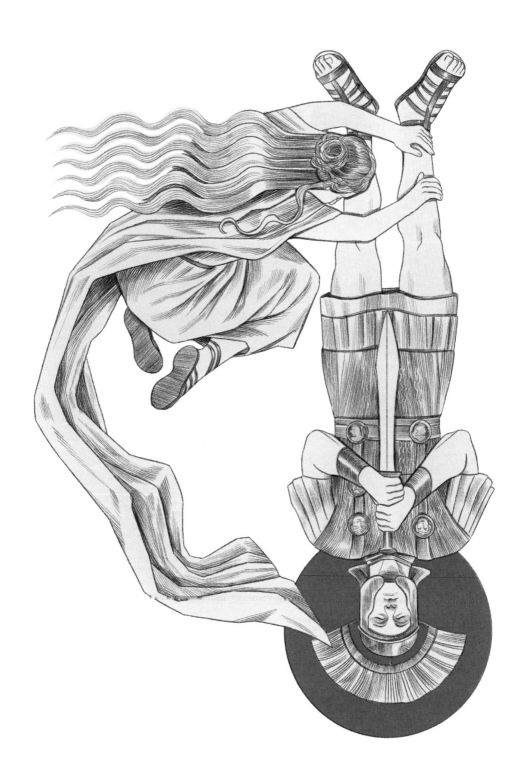

OMNIA VINCIT AMOR

MEANING: Love conquers all
ATTRIBUTION: Vergil
ORIGIN: *Eclogue* 10.69

Vergil's first work, the *Eclogues*, consists of ten poems that paint an idyllic portrait of rural life in the Roman countryside. The phrase *omnia vincit amor* is found in *Eclogue 10*, the concluding poem of the collection, in which Vergil discusses his friend, another poet, Gallus. Gallus says that "love conquers all," but it is not the rallying cry modern readers imagine. Instead, he is on his deathbed, warning us: We cannot defeat love, and so *nos cedamus*—"let us yield to it."

Gallus was an elegiac poet, or elegist. This type of poetry was new to Rome—much more contemporary than the established epic poetry, which had sewn together the fabric of Greek and Roman cultural traditions. For thousands of years, poets had wanted to emulate the Homeric poems, writing larger-than-life characters like Achilles or Odysseus. But at the end of the Roman Republic, poetry began to change. Before Vergil was commissioned to write the *Aeneid*, he pulled away from the long Greek threads that had composed epic. He wrote about men, leisure, the land, gods, the city, and love. Vergil wrote pastoral poetry, learning from poets like Catullus, Cinna, Calvus, and Cato. They were the *novi poetae*, the "new poets," and they wrote men as soldiers of love, not war.

For the elegists, love was a formidable force; it tore them up inside, often taking the form of obsession. It wasn't customary for Roman men to write about such things, nor was it acceptable for a man to be overpowered by love for a woman. Thus, the new poets parodied epic poetry by turning traditional male archetypes on their head.

In *Eclogue 10*, Gallus represents this new Roman man. Pining after his mistress while she pursues another, he embodies the *servitium amoris*—"the enslavement of love"—and his dying words admit his defeat.

SERVES ANIMAE
DIMIDIUM MEAE

MEANING: May you protect half of my soul
ATTRIBUTION: Horace
ORIGIN: *Odes* 1.3.8

An ancient Greek myth found in Plato's *Symposium* explains that humans were once impressive creatures with two heads, four arms, four legs—double everything they have now and twice as strong. Threatened by their power, Zeus decided to split all humans in half, right down the middle. He also separated the halves, producing in each a lifelong pining for its "soul mate."

Horace evokes this imagery in Ode 1.3, a *propempticon* or "bon voyage" poem addressed to Vergil's ship. The poem pleads with the vessel to ensure Vergil's safe passage along his journey to Greece, referring to him as "half of [Horace's] soul." The plea is incredibly touching and intimate, suggesting that something more than friendship—a deep, soul connection—existed between the two men. However, there is little evidence that these feelings were reciprocal. Horace addresses several poems to Vergil, but Vergil never once mentions him in return. It is clear, however, that the two men at least knew each other, as Vergil introduced Horace to their mutual patron, one of Augustus's literary ministers, Maecenas. Nevertheless, scholars continue to speculate about the true nature of their relationship.

Intense expressions of friendship were common in Roman poetry, but scholars note that this specific language was used by male poets to describe their male romantic partners. Horace finds precedent for this phrasing in the poetry of Callimachus, which describes the writer's male lover as "half of [his] soul." What's more, both Horace and Meleager, a Syrian poet writing in Greek, used sailing metaphors for homoerotic relationships. Perishing at sea was a vivid anxiety for many ancient Mediterranean people, and while Callimachus and Meleager discuss their lovers' literal demise, Horace's metaphor may warn Vergil of the dangers involved in another sort of venture: beginning to write epic poetry.

SED PECASSE IUVAT

MEANING: But it is exciting to sin
ATTRIBUTION: Sulpicia
ORIGIN: *Sulpicia* 1.9

Sulpicia is the lone extant female author writing in Latin. This line appears in the first of her six poems, in which she discusses her own erotic experiences as an upper-class Roman woman. As Sulpicia would have known, there were four main archetypes Roman women could inhabit—the maiden, the matron, the *meretrix* (literally, a sex worker, but generally, a self-sufficient woman), and the *dux femina* (a female leader)—each of which upheld the Roman patriarchy in some way. Sulpicia was the maiden: a wealthy, young, unmarried woman, whose purpose was to remain chaste in preparation for her marriage to a man.

With her taste for "sin," however, Sulpicia deviates from her prescribed role. While maidens typically proved they were ready for marriage with ostentatious displays of chastity, Sulpicia boldly proclaims her yearning, praying to Venus for her beloved to reciprocate. She uses a youthful, even spiteful tone, describing her romance with Cerinthus from its inception to its deterioration. And deteriorate it does. Her work reads as diaristic and intimate, like a modern-day teen romance:

First, Sulpicia and Cerinthus can't celebrate her birthday together; then, she discovers he's cheating. She insults the other woman, then begs to know if he worries that she might die from a fever. Eventually, she questions the point of surviving if her boyfriend doesn't care that she is sick.

We have thousands of texts mythologizing Roman womanhood, but only one from a woman herself, telling us how exciting it is to break the mold. In the end, Sulpicia's deviance did not make her more attractive to her crush, and she was ultimately rejected. This outcome would seem to support the Roman *status quo*—a feminine ideal that is meek and submissive—but the survival of her first-person account suggests a measure of victory, even by Roman standards. She may not have attained the glory promised to those who fulfilled their proper roles, but she succeeds in being remembered.

LESBIA QUID DOCUIT SAPPHO NISI AMARE PUELLAS

MEANING: What else would Lesbian Sappho teach
if not to love girls/if not girls to love?

ATTRIBUTION: Ovid

ORIGIN: *Tristia* 2.365

Although most of Sappho's poetry is now lost, the fragments that survive have become emblematic of lesbian love and desire. Indeed, the term "lesbian" itself is a reference to Sappho's birthplace at Lesbos. While the ancient Greek writer's sexuality is debated even now, in Ovid's time she was generally thought to be a lesbian in the modern sense—that is, a woman attracted to women—or perhaps a schoolteacher meant to instruct young women in how to be proper wives.

Bemoaning his life in exile, Ovid—who was banished from Rome, in part, for his sexually explicit writing—complains that other poets have written erotic material without consequence. He gives Sappho as one example, using the discourse on Sappho's sexuality to create clever wordplay. Given the ambiguous nature of the forms, the sentence can either mean: "What else would Lesbian Sappho teach if not to love girls?" or "What else would Lesbian Sappho teach if not girls to love?"

Many have criticized Latin as dull—the language of the law, accounting, and other supposedly unexciting professions. It is incredibly economical, to be sure, compressing layers of meaning into just a few words. But that efficiency paves the way for hilarious ambiguity. The most talented Latin writers expanded and contracted syllables, using the natural rhythms within words and phrases to accentuate their meaning. Or, as Ovid does here, they created double meanings by playing with subjects, verbs, and objects: *Just who is doing the loving, and of whom?*

ET AMA QUOD FEMINA DEBES

MEANING: And love how a woman should
ATTRIBUTION: Ovid
ORIGIN: *Metamorphoses* 9.748

Mythological examples of male homoeroticism abound in the ancient world, and they thrive even now, with pop culture clinging to stories of Achilles and Patroclus or Gilgamesh and Enkidu. Perhaps unsurprisingly, while a wealth of ancient poems were dedicated to male same-sex desire, little is preserved on the topic of women loving women. In the Roman conception, one's gender indicated one's sexual role—the dominator or the dominated—and there was little room for deviation, especially for women. So what about female homoeroticism? In terms of lesbians in classical mythology, they were few and far between. In fact, there is only one known classical mythological account of female same-sex desire: Ovid's myth of Iphis and Ianthe.

A poor Cretan father-to-be tells his pregnant wife that if their baby is a girl, they must leave her to die. The wife cannot bear to kill her newborn, so she dresses her daughter as a boy and gives her the gender-neutral name Iphis. Iphis is raised as a boy, but her femaleness becomes difficult to conceal during puberty. Nevertheless, Iphis meets Ianthe, another Cretan girl, and they are engaged. Iphis is conflicted and commands herself to "love as a woman *should*"—that is, to love a man. She looks to the natural world to make her case: "Heifer does not love heifer, nor does mare love mare." When, just before her wedding, Iphis is in danger of being discovered, the goddess Isis physically transforms her into a man, and the ceremony continues as planned.

Many incorrectly argue that gender and sexuality are modern inventions; however, the ancient world was obviously intrigued by gender. Today, scholars do not agree on Iphis's self-identification, either as a heterosexual transgender man or as a homosexual cisgender woman. But if Iphis is marked by how a woman should *not* love, then the inverse must be true: a woman, in Roman society, is defined as someone who loves a man.

INVISUS NATALIS ADEST

MEANING: My annoying birthday is here
ATTRIBUTION: Sulpicia
ORIGIN: *Sulpicia* 2.1

A sullen Sulpicia complains about her birthday, lamenting not her age but where she will have to spend the occasion. In Sulpicia's short poem, she details her birthday grievances: Her uncle Messalla is forcing her to spend the day away from Rome and, most annoyingly, away from her boyfriend, Cerinthus. Sulpicia complains about the countryside because, she writes, *"dulcius urbe quid est?"*—what's sweeter than the city? Farms are no place for a young girl; they are freezing cold and rustic.

Though the poem focuses on Sulpicia's likes and dislikes, it also reveals biographical details that may indicate the true nature of her frustration. Interestingly, it is not Sulpicia's father who forces her to the countryside but her uncle, Messalla. His unilateral decision suggests that Sulpicia is unmarried and her father has died, granting Messalla *patris potestas*—the power of a father. This included legal and social privileges such as the right to sell your children into slavery, make decisions regarding marriages, and enact capital punishment. In Rome, even fatherless daughters could not escape patriarchal control. In fact, the only women exempt from *patris potestas* were the Vestal Virgins—young women who were chosen as priestesses for the goddess Vesta. By pledging chastity, they rendered themselves "free." Unable to swear this oath, Sulpicia can only grumble. When she ends her poem with the line, directed at Messalla, *"arbitrio quamvis non sinis esse meo"*—you don't allow whatever my judgment is—one imagines her anger runs deeper than birthday woes.

SOROR ANIMA

MEANING: Soul sister
ATTRIBUTION: Claudia Severa
ORIGIN: Vindolanda Tablet 291

Where women's voices survive, they illuminate spheres of life otherwise poorly documented or understood. For example, the Vindolanda tablets—a set of wooden tablets found at a military fort in former Roman Britain—offer a look inside the daily life of a woman in a military encampment. The oldest surviving Latin text attributed to a woman, the document is a letter from a fort commander's wife, Claudia Severa, inviting her friend to a birthday party. The tone is warm; the women knew each other well and had clearly been to each other's homes several times in the past. Claudia Severa likely dictated her invitation to a scribe, but in her own handwriting, she adds a personalized note: "I will expect you, sister; goodbye, soul sister."

Although not poetic, Claudia Severa's closing alludes to a sisterhood described in Vergil's *Aeneid*:

Aeneas and the other Trojans take refuge by invitation of Dido, the founding queen of the African city of Carthage. Aeneas and Dido marry, but ultimately, the gods intervene, pushing Aeneas to establish a new empire in Rome. Dido is devastated when she sees the Trojan ships leaving. She begs her sister, Anna, "with whom (she) share(s) a soul," to build a pyre taller than the city skyline. Anna obliges, believing that Dido plans to perform a strange ritual, not realizing she is building her funeral pyre. Dido then climbs atop the pyre and stabs herself with the Trojan sword Aeneas left behind.

While today, "soul sister" is a simple term of endearment, in Claudia Severa's time, it would have implied the closeness and trust shared by Dido and Anna. Dido's request of Anna, though veiled, is an incredibly intimate one. She asks her sister to release her from her heartbreak.

HIC VITAM TRIBUIT
SED HIC AMICUM

MEANING: [My birthday] gave me my life, but yours, a friend
ATTRIBUTION: Martial
ORIGIN: *Epigrams* 9.52.6-7

Roman authors devised a million ways to say "I love you," and the birthday poem was one. Often composed as gifts, these poems were expressions of deep affection. Martial addresses his friend, Quintus Ovidius: "If you believe me, I love your April birthday as much as I love mine in March." Quintus's birthday, Martial says, "gave [him] more" than life: "it provided a friend."

Martial's sweetness here indicates how seriously birthdays were taken in Rome. His concise poems—called epigrams—are well known for being incredibly raunchy, rife with the sort of sexual innuendos young Latin students now whisper giddily. But celebrating a birthday other than one's own was a formal event. Even if he did not physically attend a friend's birthday party, a Roman might honor the occasion individually by performing certain rituals—or by penning a poetic expression of love.

ODI ET AMO

MEANING: I hate, and I love
ATTRIBUTION: Catullus
ORIGIN: Catullus 85

In one of his most iconic and memorable poems, Catullus examines the fickle nature of relationships: "I hate, and I love. Why do I do this? / I don't know, but I feel it happening, and I'm tortured."

Catullus, an atypically melancholic poet, died at the young age of thirty. He was born into an equestrian family, a wealth class with a minimum property requirement of 400,000 sesterces, or more than two million U.S. dollars. He spent one year on a governor's staff but did not entertain a political or military career, as would have been expected for a Roman of his class. Nevertheless, he engaged with influential literary and political figures in the late Roman Republic, such as Julius Caesar, the historian Asinius Pollio, and the biographer Cornelius Nepos. He was also influential in his own right, uplifting Greek Callimachaean aesthetics in Rome, affecting a departure from traditional epic.

Catullus includes several biographical details in his poetry, famously discussing at length his affair with a woman named Lesbia. A pseudonym, "Lesbia" was likely a reference to Sappho; it may have been chosen to convey that this woman was also a poet, or that she, too, was from Lesbos. In any case, Catullus was tortured by his affection for her. Within the short poem, it seems that he might be asking himself a rhetorical question: *Why do I feel this way?* But in the dozens of poems preceding, he is excessively clear about his mercurial affair with Lesbia, a younger married woman who can commit neither to her marriage nor her affair.

Though Catullus certainly was not lucky in love, he excelled in terms of longevity; his works are still used in Latin classrooms today, mainly for their brevity, but also for their shock value. Openly emotive and introspective, Catullus's style differed considerably from that of his predecessors. It ushered in a new era for Roman poets, led by the *novi poetae*—young, typically wealthy men who wrote not of war and politics, but of love.

VESTALES NOSTRAS HODIE CREDIMUS

MEANING: Even today, we believe our Vestal Virgins
ATTRIBUTION: Pliny the Elder
ORIGIN: *Natural Histories* 28.3

The success of Rome depended on its people's adherence to strict moral values. Men followed the *mos maiorum*—the way of the ancestors—espousing *fides* (faithfulness), *virtus* (uprightness), and *pietas* (dutifulness). Women were also expected to adhere to *fides*, but according to different standards. For them, faithfulness meant either remaining virgins until marriage and committing to monogamy as wives or serving as priestesses in the state-sponsored religion.

The cult of Vesta, the goddess of the hearth and, therefore, of family life, protected the Eternal Flame of Rome, which represented the city's prosperity. Were the flame to go out, it portended Rome's destruction—and it meant that one of the Vestal Virgins who guarded the flame had not remained chaste. There were six Vestal Virgins at any given time. Appointed as children between the ages of six and ten, these women served thirty-year terms during which they were expected to remain virginal. In exchange, they received special freedoms and privileges, like front row seats at the Coliseum and a pension following their service. However, if a Vestal Virgin failed to keep her oath, she would be carried through the streets on a funeral bed and buried alive in a small chamber.

Though the priestesshood was established during the early Roman monarchy, the custom lasted until the fourth century CE. In his encyclopedia, the *Natural Histories*, Pliny the Elder questions the efficacy of old curses, charms, and prayers. Ultimately, he concludes that such practices are legitimate, citing the obvious power of the Vestal Virgins. With the recitation of a particular prayer, these holy women could, among other things, "arrest the flight of runaway slaves."

Though clearly some doubt existed regarding magic, charms, and curses, Romans held ancestral tradition in high regard.

MYTHOLOGY

"IT WAS NOT CREATED OUT OF THE EMPTY AIR BUT OUT OF
THE LONG TRADITION OF STORYTELLING, OUT OF MYTH."

–Ralph Ellison

LUPUS IN FABULA

MEANING: The wolf in the story
ATTRIBUTION: Terence
ORIGIN: *Adelphoe* 4.1

In Terence's palliata *Adelphoe*, Ctesipho and Syrus are conspiring against Demea when, suddenly, he appears. "*Lupus in fabula!*" Syrus exclaims. Much like the English idiom "Speak of the devil," this phrase was uttered when the subject of conversation—a person, most often—entered unexpectedly, almost as though summoned. The exclamation appears in several Roman texts, not just plays but poetry and prose, suggesting its use was widespread.

The wolf was an important symbol for Romans, central to many myths, but perhaps most notably, that of the founding of Rome. The tale appears in Livy's *Ab Urbe Condita*:

A Vestal Virgin, Rhea Silvia, is raped by the god Mars and becomes pregnant. Her oath of chastity now broken, she is allowed to give birth before she is buried alive, and her twin sons, Romulus and Remus, are left in the wilderness to die. A vicious female wolf begins to stalk the infants, but rather than pounce, she suckles them back to health. Eventually, a shepherd discovers the twins deep in the forest and brings them home to raise with his wife.

Years later, Romulus and Remus discover their noble parentage and decide to seek out some land to rule over. Happening upon a spot with seven hills, the brothers disagree about where to settle. They resolve the dispute through augury. Remus says he sees six birds fly past, but Romulus, perhaps deceitfully, claims to have seen twelve, "winning" the divination. A jilted Remus insults Romulus's choice, and a skirmish breaks out, resulting in Remus's death.

Depending on your perspective, the story can be interpreted as one of mercy and salvation—two innocent boys rescued against all odds—or as one of death and betrayal—a vile fratricide. Regardless, "the wolf in the story" is pivotal; her entrance marks a moment of tension: Will she pounce? Likely. Or will she inexplicably exercise mercy?

MANUS MANUM LAVAT

MEANING: One hand washes the other hand
ATTRIBUTION: Seneca the Younger
ORIGIN: *Apocolocyntosis* 9

In a satire, Seneca tells of Claudius's death and ascension to Mount Olympus, where, like all former emperors, he will face judgment from the gods. The work's title, *Apocolocyntosis*, literally means "Pumpkinification" and is a play on the term *apotheosis*—the process by which one becomes a god after death. Scholars disagree about the exact nature of Seneca's joke here, but it's clear he intended to mock Claudius.

Several gods give speeches rejecting Claudius, including the former-emperor-turned-god, Augustus. They accuse him of gambling, accepting bribes, and lacking self-control or a way with words. They characterize him as a tyrant and criticize his legal decision-making skills. They even critique his mobility impairment, speech impediment, and tics. Seneca was primarily a Stoic philosopher, and by that token, he likely would have seen physical disability and mental illness as reflective of some moral deficiency.

However, there is one prominent dissenter: Hercules. Because several pages of the satire are missing, it's unclear why Hercules was moved to defend Claudius or even whether he ultimately held to his position. But in the course of his speech, Hercules attempts to bargain with other gods for support. "*Manus manum lavat*," he says, or, "one hand washes the other hand," meaning, essentially, that if they side with him on this matter, Hercules will do the same for them when the time comes. The phrase is similar to the more common Medieval Latin expression *quid pro quo*, which puts the sentiment more directly: "this for that."

Ultimately, Claudius does not become a god. Instead, he is escorted to the Underworld, where he is sentenced to endure various humiliating punishments. Although Claudius is characterized as a gambler, it is Hercules—a god—who attempts a bribe on his behalf. One can only "wash the other (hand)" if one has power and influence.

QUID SI COMANTUR?

MEANING: What if (her hair) was combed?

ATTRIBUTION: Ovid

ORIGIN: *Metamorphoses* 1.498

In his influential *Metamorphoses*, Ovid recounts the myth of Apollo and Daphne:

Insulted by Apollo, Cupid seeks revenge by shooting two arrows: one, made of gold, strikes Apollo, filling him with insatiable lust, and the other, made of lead, pierces the unlucky nymph Daphne, causing her to flee any lover. Daphne, who has been promised eternal virginity by her father, runs from the lovestruck Apollo, tearing through forest thickets where no path has yet been formed. Her feet barely touch the ground and make almost no sound. Thorns scratch her bare legs as she passes, but she continues, never turning her head to see who chases her. Suddenly, an awful noise breaks the silence. It is the amorous Apollo, exclaiming of Daphne's wild hair: "What if it was combed?"

The comment, though humorous to modern ears, compounds Daphne's shame. Long, flowing hair was a mark of beauty, and Daphne's, though tangled, had cursed her. What if she could be rid of it? The nymph prays to her father—a river god—pleading with him to "destroy (her) beauty."

Just as Apollo catches up to Daphne, her transformation begins: her arms and legs solidify, her hair turns to leafy branches, and what was once her torso forms a wooden trunk. Undeterred, Apollo caresses her bark, declaring her, if not his wife, then his prized tree. He clips a piece of her "hair"—the laurel wreath—and with it, he vows to crown future champions.

Though mythical, the story illustrates a real-life dilemma familiar to Roman women. If she wished to avoid marriage, what options did a woman have? She would need the protection of her father. But even then, if she were beautiful, men would still try to claim her. The better defense, it seems, was to subvert established beauty standards. In the end, Daphne's uncombed hair could not save her, but Apollo's *"quid si comantur"* suggests it might have, were Cupid's arrow not in play.

Neque semper arcum tendit Apollo

MEANING: Apollo does not always stretch his bow
ATTRIBUTION: Horace
ORIGIN: *Odes* 2.10.19-20

M oderatio, or moderation, was an important Roman value included in the *mos maiorum*, along with piety, faithfulness, and uprightness. In his so-called "golden mean" poem, Horace advises a friend on how to live moderately, pointing out that even vengeful gods practice self-control.

Horace's view is reflective of Roman Epicureanism, which valued balance and looked for pleasure in restraint. Epicureans resisted what they thought to be a needless fear of the gods, whom they believed were neutral— neither good nor evil.

Take Apollo, for example: the ruler of sickness and health, inspiration and profanity, the rural and the urban. He teaches that pain always accompanies beauty, and in this way, even Apollo practices moderation. He may have once rained plague on Trojan shores, but he does not hold his bow taut. That is, he does not always enact wrath on mortal men.

Aspiring to such a "mean," Horace advises, isn't cowardly, but godlike.

Equo ne credite, timeo danaos et dona ferentes

MEANING: Don't trust the horse . . . I fear the Greeks, even those bringing gifts

ATTRIBUTION: Vergil

ORIGIN: *Aeneid* 2.48-49

In the second book of the *Aeneid*, Aeneas regales the Phoenicians with his story of the final siege on Troy:

To end the ten-year Trojan War, the Greek strategist Odysseus plans to give the Trojans a gift they cannot refuse. Feigning retreat, the Greeks leave a hollow wooden horse on the Trojan shore as a peace offering. Packed tightly with Greek warriors, the "gift" is, of course, a ruse. Once it is wheeled inside the well-braced walls of Troy, the hidden soldiers will emerge, decimating their longtime foes.

But before this happens, the Trojan priest Laocoön approaches the gift horse suspiciously. He pierces the wood with his spear, producing a rattling sound. "Don't trust the horse!" he cautions. Angered by Laocoön's cleverness, the gods retaliate, sending snakes to eat him and his twin sons.

While Laocoön's swift demise should have confirmed the Greeks' deceit, it has the opposite effect: the Trojans interpret it as proof of the priest's foolishness, and they accept the fateful gift. Perhaps to heighten the foreboding of Laocoön's death, Vergil lingers over the scene, using consonance and alliteration to simulate snakes slithering close. While the repeated "s" sounds are conspicuous in English, in Latin, the words flow together perfectly, mimicking both hissing snakes and the rolling of waves onto the Trojan shore.

While Laocoön himself is hardly remembered, if the story of the Trojan horse has a moral, it is contained in his words "*Equo ne credite*," that is, beware your enemy, even—and perhaps especially—if they offer enticing gifts.

BELLA GERANT ALII PROTESILAUS AMET!

MEANING: Let others wage war—Protesilaus should love!
ATTRIBUTION: Ovid
ORIGIN: *Heroides* 13.82

Ovid's *Heroides*, or the Heroines, is a collection of letters written from the perspective of famous mythological women. Ovid claims to have invented this genre: the rhetorical dance of imagining what women would say—if they could.

In *Heroides* 13, Ovid inhabits the perspective of Laodamia, writing to her husband, Protesilaus, who has been asked by Menelaus and Odysseus to fight in the Trojan War. She urges him not to go, claiming that he is better suited to love than to battle. Plenty of fame-hungry men will volunteer to fight, she says. Let them spill their blood for others' causes, but not dear Protesilaus: "Protesilaus should love!"

Laodamia's pleas are in vain. As Ovid's readers would have known, the Oracle had foretold that the first Greek soldier to touch Trojan soil would be the first to perish. And perish Protesilaus would, leaping eagerly from his ship onto cursed Trojan shores.

The Trojan War was an especially long and violent conflict. For the soldiers, a death in battle promised glory, but for the wives, mothers, and daughters they left behind, there was little consolation. Although Laodamia could not have known her husband's fate, she seems to intuit it. Like the Oracle, she has wisdom to offer, but being mortal—and a woman at that—she can only beg and entreat.

Igitur censuit Asinius Gallus ut libri Sibyllini adirentur

MEANING: Thus, Asinius Gallus suggested that the
Sibylline Books be consulted

ATTRIBUTION: Tacitus

ORIGIN: *Annales* 1.76

The Sibylline Books were a collection of prophecies made by Sibyls—women who were said to have been blessed by Apollo with psychic abilities. According to legend, the Books were acquired by the last king of Rome, Tarquinius Superbus, and were consulted during public crises such as plagues, wars, and natural disasters. True or not, the Books were a powerful tool for Roman politicians.

In the *Annals*—a record of major events—the historian Tacitus writes that during the reign of Rome's second emperor, Tiberius, the Tiber River flooded catastrophically. To determine how to proceed, Asinius Gallus, a senator, recommended that the emperor consult the Sibylline Books, but Tiberius refused. Instead, he appointed two men to devise a plan to confine the river. This proved a disastrous mistake. Ultimately, the men failed at their task, as they were unable to appease both divinity and the townspeople. Clearly disapproving of Tiberius's arrogance, Tacitus characterized the emperor as a deceitful tyrant.

Today, we think of history as a collection of immutable facts and dates, but Roman historiography was a broad genre that included etiology: the study of mythical explanations for phenomena. Historians like Tacitus were concerned both with the recording of events and the role of divinity in their unfolding.

Is Venerem e Rapido
Sentiet Esse Mari

MEANING: She is like Venus, born from blood and an angry sea
ATTRIBUTION: Tibullus
ORIGIN: Tibullus 1.2.42

Romans were concerned with creating order out of chaos, and their poetry mimicked that tendency, arranged just so by its careful stewards. Not Tibullus. His poetry embraced the chaos, and perhaps for that reason, modern scholarship largely ignores it.

Unsurprisingly, Tibullus lived during one of Rome's most tumultuous periods. Born between 60 and 55 BCE, he would have been old enough to remember Caesar's assassination, the fall of the Republic, and the entirety of Augustus's reign. But his poetry doesn't touch those topics. Instead, it centers on Delia, his mistress. While Tibullus is vague about Delia's social station, he often describes her begging him for gifts and favors, indicating that she is likely a *meretrix*—a sex worker.

This line comes from Tibullus's most well-known poem, a *paraclausithyron*, a Greek word meaning "to lament outside a door." Tibullus is inebriated, wailing outside the home of Delia's much-wealthier lover. He begs the door of the house to open, allowing him to see Delia in person. When the door does not oblige, Tibullus turns his attention to Venus, goddess of love, praising her and asking her to persuade Delia to sneak out of bed. Tibullus claims that Venus will protect Delia, allowing her to escape undetected, and that anyone who sees them together will fall silent or face the wrath of a goddess "born from blood and an angry sea." Here, Tibullus references the story of Venus's birth. According to myth, the goddess sauntered out of the ocean a fully grown adult, sprung from the "sea foam" of Uranus's severed genitals.

Though vivid, the threat falls flat. By invoking the image of a famous castration, Tibullus—who has already degraded himself by begging for the help of a door—reminds readers of his impotence. The line evidences his literary talents, but its complexity seals his modern obscurity.

MILITARY
AND POWER

"PUSHED, THEY FALL. FALLEN, THEY LIE WHERE
THEY ARE, UNLESS CHANCE GIVES SOMEBODY
THE IDEA OF RAISING THEM UP AGAIN."

–Simone Weil

TENEO TE AFRICA

MEANING: I am holding you, Africa
ATTRIBUTION: Julius Caesar via Suetonius
ORIGIN: *Divus Julius 59.1*

O n his first journey to Africa, Julius Caesar fell flat on his face—literally. He tripped as he disembarked his boat. Knowing the stumble would be perceived as a bad omen for his military campaign, he attempted to transform it into an intentional gesture. He grasped at the earth with his fists and announced, "I am holding you, Africa."

Omens were significant to Romans. Much of their political system was based on readings by augurs—men who observed birds and interpreted their flight patterns as divine messages. Augurs posed strict yes-or-no questions to the gods: "Do you approve of this?" Thus, the results of an augury could only be favorable or unfavorable.

As the *pontifex maximus*, the "supreme priest" charged with managing the augurs, Caesar needed to ensure that his actions indicated the gods' favor. Of course, scholars aren't sure what tone Caesar used—whether he meant to poke fun at himself or take his position seriously. What's certain is that although Caesar held considerable religious and political power, he still embarrassed himself as humans do.

CARTHAGO DELENDA EST

MEANING: Carthage must be destroyed
ATTRIBUTION: Cato the Elder
ORIGIN: Various speeches

Cato the Elder was a Roman politician in the second century BCE who advocated for a return to "traditional" Roman values and anti-Hellenization. He was particularly well-known for ending each of his senatorial speeches by calling for the destruction of Carthage—at the time, Rome's most formidable rival and a competitor for control over Sicily.

The Punic Wars between Rome and Carthage had begun before Cato the Elder's birth and raged on for three years following his death. Over the course of his senatorial career, and fearing the prosperity of Carthage, Cato called for Roman intervention following two previous wars that had diminished, but not destroyed, the African city. Though Cato the Elder did not live to see Carthage fall, his repeated exhortation was eventually fulfilled. In this final war, Rome obliterated Carthage and took control of all Carthaginian territories, establishing the Roman province of Africa.

Modern-day political campaigns take their cue from Cato, who clearly understood the power of an easily remembered phrase, repeated *ad nauseam*. Today, however, such "slogans" are often intentionally vague—leaving reasonable doubt as to whether they intend to incite violence. For Cato, however, the call to destroy Carthage was sincere and its fulfillment, in his mind, essential.

IMPERIUM SINE FINE

MEANING: Power without end
ATTRIBUTION: Vergil
ORIGIN: *Aeneid* 1.279

In Vergil's *Aeneid*, the titular protagonist, Aeneas, was a Trojan War refugee. Following the Greeks' brutal surprise attack, he fled the city of his birth, carrying his elderly father and infant son on his back. Tearfully, he looked back at his home, barely able to see through the thick flames that engulfed the once-mighty city. Though he had lost nearly everything, he trusted the gods when they said he had a duty to fulfill: to reach Italy, where his descendants would one day establish the city of Rome.

Aeneas could hardly fathom surviving the journey, particularly the harsh sea storms. His divine mother, Venus, the goddess of love and sexuality, begged Jupiter to end Aeneas's suffering. Jupiter, the king of the gods, did not do so but offered indirect relief in the form of a divine mandate: With Aeneas's fate fulfilled, the future Romans would have *imperium sine fine*—power without end.

Aeneas had the opportunity to establish a new type of city—one like Carthage, where the Tyrian refugees worked together, hivelike, to rebuild their society. Yet violence begets violence, and brutality creates brutalists: more men willing to conquer, deface, and burn. Even after experiencing war and displacement at the hands of the Greeks, Aeneas would inflict the same horrors on the indigenous Latians who inhabited the land that would eventually be called Rome.

For modern readers, *imperium* might evoke its cognate, "empire," and while the original Latin did not refer to a geographic boundary, it did imply a vastness of power. The so-called crusade of "power without end" has been taken up by cultures throughout history and around the globe—with disastrous results.

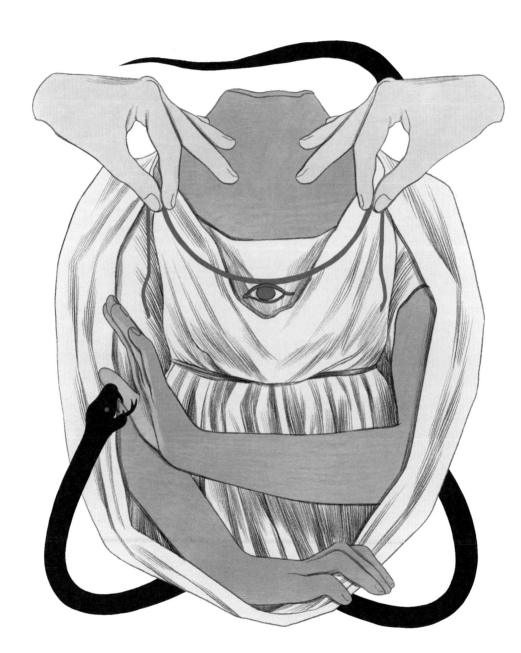

ABSIT INVIDIA

MEANING: Let jealousy be absent
ATTRIBUTION: Livy
ORIGIN: *Ab Urbe Condita* 9.19.15

To protect against the "evil eye"—a curse thought to emanate from an envious glare—Romans performed various rituals; some carried a phallic talisman called a *fascinum* to deflect potential misfortune, injury, or even death.

In Livy's seminal work of Roman historiography, *Ab Urbe Condita*, he employs a common verbal defense against the curse. Discussing Alexander the Great, a general who expanded the Greek empire from Egypt to India, Livy is not impressed. Somewhat boastfully, he claims that if Alexander had tried to conquer Italy, Rome would have defeated him. Given Alexander's impressive record of conquest and considerable fame during Livy's lifetime, this statement would have seemed excessive—even delusional. Livy must have known this, because he follows it with "let jealousy be absent."

In Rome, boasting in any form was to be avoided, for it might incite *invidia*, or envy, which was associated with dangerous magic. The evil eye concept still exists today in a number of cultures. While modern believers carry talismans for protection, others wear them decoratively—perhaps tempting a jealous glance.

ALEA IACTA EST

MEANING: The die has been cast
ATTRIBUTION: Julius Caesar via Suetonius
ORIGIN: *Divus Julius* 32.1

According to the imperial biographer Suetonius, Julius Caesar spoke these words as he crossed the Rubicon River with his army in a symbolic declaration of civil war. The Rubicon formed part of the *pomerium*, a religious boundary that encircled Rome and its territories. Romulus was said to have carved this sacred boundary himself when he built the walls of the original city, marking a perimeter beyond which certain "impurities" could not pass. Corpses, weapons, and capital punishment were all prohibited within the *pomerium*. Therefore, when Caesar crossed the Rubicon with his armed soldiers, he committed a ritual assault against his own people.

Ancient historians disagree on the exact phrasing and context of Caesar's statement. While Suetonius claims that Caesar was inspired by an ominous trumpeter across the river, the historian Plutarch contradicts himself in two different accounts: In one, he claims Caesar rushed forth across the Rubicon, but in another, he says he "stood in silence, and delayed crossing, reasoning with himself." Whether hurried or hesitant, Caesar characterizes his actions as beyond his control. While today dice are associated with gambling and probability, in ancient Rome the results of a dice game were thought to be predestined. So when Caesar crosses the Rubicon, the move may be out of his hands, but it is not random; it's in accordance with his Fate.

Sub iugum mittere

MEANING: To send under the yoke
ATTRIBUTION: Julius Caesar
ORIGIN: *De Bello Gallico* 1.12

Roman military tacticians are famed for their war victories—and their elaborate rituals. In one of Julius Caesar's autobiographies, *De Bello Gallico*, he details several Roman wartime customs, including *sub iugum mittere*—a ritual that stands out for its religious significance.

After the Romans had defeated an army in battle, they would typically either free or enslave the captured enemies. Though the Roman economy would eventually thrive on forced labor, during the Roman Kingdom a formal system of enslavement had not yet been established. It was also costly to feed and guard the captives before they could be brought into the city and sold. Most often, they were released. But before the enemy soldiers could flee, they were "sent under the yoke" in a ritual meant to cleanse them of the bloodguilt they had incurred on the battlefield. Because they had shed the blood of fellow men, the soldiers' own blood was considered polluted or foul (*foedus*).

Passing under the yoke was a ritual of both mercy and humiliation. Captives were stripped of their clothing and covered in dirt, blood, and grime before being forced to crawl on their knees. The Romans planted two spears in the ground and tied one horizontally across, forming a low archway. The semi-nude soldiers were then made to pass beneath the horizontal spear, bowing as they did. In later artistic depictions, a literal yoke was used, implying further shame and degradation. This practice was a rite of passage, intended to move the soldiers from the realm of the profane (*profanum*) into that of the sacred (*sacrum*).

To address their own bloodguilt, Roman soldiers endured a far more dignified cleansing, passing through the *Campus Martius*, the Field of Mars, before their arrival into the city.

In fluvium primi cecidere, in corpora summi

MEANING: First, they were thrown in the river, then on top of bodies
ATTRIBUTION: Lucan
ORIGIN: *Pharsalia* 2.211

The poet Lucan could be described as Vergil's stylistic opposite; whereas Vergil was slow and deliberate in crafting his verse, Lucan was quick and rash. The grandson of Seneca the Elder and author of an unfinished epic poem, the *Pharsalia*, about Caesar's Civil War, Lucan never knew a republic—only an ever-expanding empire.

Lucan initially found success under Nero's reign; however, the two fell out. While historians debate the reason for the rupture, Lucan may have turned against Nero amidst speculation that the emperor had caused the Great Fire of Rome, a weeklong blaze during which more than two-thirds of the city was destroyed. Rumors flew about Nero's role in the disaster, including that he had ordered the *vigiles*—the Roman fire brigade—to allow the fire to rage, and that he had played a lyre while the city burned, razing the ground for his future palace, the *Domus Aurea*. These stories and others like them spiraled out of control, and Nero lost his already tenuous grip on the public favor.

The *Pharsalia*, though not *about* Nero, indirectly conveys Lucan's changing feelings toward the emperor. Book 1, which scholars believe was written before Nero's corruption was exposed, is dedicated to him. But Lucan's tone quickly becomes anti-Julio-Claudian. He depicts the civil war between the bellicose Julius Caesar and Pompey as offensively gruesome: bodies were "thrown in the river, then on top of other bodies," meaning bodies were piled high and allowed to pollute the sacred river with their uncleansed blood. In later books, written as Nero's image devolved, Lucan's tone is increasingly anti-imperial.

Along with his uncle, Seneca the Younger, and the satirist Petronius, Lucan eventually joined a conspiracy to assassinate Nero. When it failed, these men, whose literary accomplishments Nero had once celebrated, were forced to commit suicide. Lucan was only twenty-five years old.

DULCE ET DECORUM EST PRO PATRIA MORI

MEANING: It is sweet and honorable to die for your country

ATTRIBUTION: Horace

ORIGIN: *Odes* 3.2.13

W ords were not the only weapon of the poet Horace; during one of many Roman civil wars, he took up arms. The freeborn son of a tax collector, Horace left Rome for Athens as a young adult, enrolling in the Academy, the famous school founded by Plato in the fourth century BCE. While there, he was among the educated young men recruited by Brutus to become high-ranking soldiers. With his fellow pupils, Horace learned to fight in the Greek wildlands as a member of Brutus's army.

When Marc Antony and Octavian ultimately defeated Brutus in the Battle of Philippi, Octavian offered clemency to his opponents, including Horace. But when Horace returned to Rome, he found that his late father's estate had been seized for land redistribution. With no money or prospects, he turned to writing poetry. Though it was not a lucrative career, Horace hoped that writing would give him access to other poets' wealthy patrons.

Sure enough, Horace gained favor with Maecenas, Octavian's literary minister, and became enmeshed in the new government he had fought against in the civil war. But being Maecenas's client put Horace in a politically precarious position. To protect himself, he began to write poetry in support of Augustus's political vision, which included the idea that it was "sweet and honorable" to die for Rome.

Centuries later, the modern British poet and soldier Wilfred Owen would refer in his own poem to Horace's line as "the old lie"—and in a sense, that's precisely what it was. It was Augustus's lie, but it was also Horace's—penned in an effort to advance his career.

ODERINT DUM METUANT

MEANING: Let them hate as long as they fear
ATTRIBUTION: Caligula via Suetonius
ORIGIN: *Caligula* 30

The third Roman emperor, Caligula, was well-regarded during the early months of his reign, but after an unexpected illness, he began to behave erratically, carrying out sadistic killings. In his biography of the emperor, Suetonius reports that once, "through a mistake in the names," Caligula executed the wrong man. Not only did he express no remorse for his error, he also claimed that the victim had deserved it. "Let them hate as long as they fear," he added, quoting the poet Accius.

But Caligula's decisions were not merely fearsome, they were increasingly unhinged. He made his horse a consul, for example, and stormed the beaches of Britannia, commanding soldiers to collect seashells. Eventually, he claimed he was divine and ordered that statues of the gods have their heads replaced with his own.

Ultimately, Caligula must have overestimated the degree to which he was feared, because those who hated him became his assassins. Perhaps unsurprisingly, officers in the Praetorian Guard, the emperor's bodyguards, conspired to assassinate Caligula and succeeded.

Though the young emperor's story should serve as a cautionary tale, dozens of power-hungry rulers have followed Caligula's example, reigning through terror—and many of those have met his same end.

AUT VIAM INVENIAM AUT FACIAM

MEANING: Either I'll find a way, or I'll make one
ATTRIBUTION: Hannibal Barca
ORIGIN: Unknown

Born in Carthage (present-day Tunis, Tunisia), the general Hannibal Barca had been preparing for war with Rome from the time he could hold a spear. When the opportunity arose, he was unstoppable. Knowing he could not defeat the Roman navy, he strategically avoided a marine battle by crossing the Alps—with elephants. When faced with the impossible task, Hannibal allegedly declared his determination: "Either I'll find a way, or I'll make one." And so he did. According to Livy, the journey through the Alps took only sixteen days. When the elephants were initially unable to pass through the freezing slopes, Hannibal commanded his engineers to dig a narrow road out of the rubble. Three days later, the passage was wide enough for the elephants. Though the animals and soldiers suffered from severe hunger, they successfully traversed the mountains, maintaining their surprise advantage, and defeated the Romans at the Battle of Cannae.

According to Vergil's *Aeneid*, the feud between Carthage and Rome was inherited from the gods. The goddess Juno hated Aeneas, as she knew he would eventually oppose her favorite city, Carthage. The Carthaginian queen Dido wed Aeneas, and the two planned to rule jointly. But Aeneas was destined to land in Italy. He abandoned Dido, leaving her to burn. The conflict began there: two lovers separated by fate, and a queen's heartbroken demise. Their cities were fated to spar.

Hannibal, it would seem, was as bound by duty as Aeneas. The latest in a long line of Carthaginian generals willing to die to defeat Rome, he did "make (his) way," but to limited effect. The Carthaginian senate did not throw its support behind Hannibal's tactics, and he was ultimately defeated at the Battle of Zama, ending the Second Punic War. Nevertheless, he is celebrated as one of the greatest generals of all time.

CULTURE AND PHILOSOPHY

"SCHOOL HOUSES DO NOT TEACH THEMSELVES–PILES OF
BRICK AND MORTAR AND MACHINERY DO NOT SEND OUT
MEN. IT IS THE TRAINED, LIVING HUMAN SOUL, CULTIVATED
AND STRENGTHENED BY LONG STUDY AND THOUGHT,
THAT BREATHES THE REAL BREATH OF LIFE INTO BOYS
AND GIRLS AND MAKES THEM HUMAN, WHETHER THEY
BE BLACK OR WHITE, GREEK, RUSSIAN OR AMERICAN."

–W. E. B. Du Bois

MEMENTO MORI

MEANING: Remember you will die
ATTRIBUTION: Contested
ORIGIN: Roman Proverb

Writing in the voice of Socrates, Plato claimed that the goal of philosophy was to practice dying and being dead. Death, for Plato, was defined as the separation of the body from the soul. Therefore, the living man could come nearest truth—to ideas in their purest form—by "playing dead," so to speak: by denying the physical body, its attending pleasures and desires.

While the Roman Stoics did not conceive of the body and soul exactly as Plato did, they agreed that death involved the separation of the two and that, in confronting death, men could achieve freedom. The fear of death, for the Stoics, was ultimately futile, and it interfered with living a virtuous and meaningful life. Meaning blossomed from an awareness of death, which motivated one to prioritize life and waste no time. Stoic philosophers' words on this theme remain. For Seneca, Marcus Aurelius, and Epictetus, each day was a profound gift and not to be taken for granted.

To emphasize this, during the Republic, Roman slaves were tasked with whispering *memento mori* in the ears of generals during the triumphal procession, reminding them, "You may be adored as a god now, but remember, you will die as a human does." The phrase was also adopted by early Christians. Because their rewards lay beyond death in the kingdom of Heaven, Christians were mindful of their mortality, "practicing death" by living without the world's vanities.

FORTES FORTUNA IUVAT

MEANING: Fortune favors the brave
ATTRIBUTION: Pliny the Elder via Pliny the Younger
ORIGIN: *Epistulae 6.16.11*

In a letter written to the historian Tacitus, Pliny the Younger describes the actions of his uncle, Pliny the Elder, in the wake of the Vesuvian eruption of 79 CE. Pliny the Elder, who was the commanding officer of a port city near Pompeii, launched a rescue mission with his naval fleet. In response to the suggestion that his fleet turn back, Pliny allegedly insisted: "Fortune favors the brave."

As Pliny and his crew arrived ashore in Herculaneum—a smaller city even nearer Vesuvius than Pompeii—sheets of pumice and ash rained down from the sky. An accomplished naturalist, Pliny likely understood the danger he was in. He may also have foreseen the perils to come: earthquakes, tsunamis, and aftershocks. Still, he led his men into the city. The group lodged at the home of Pliny's friend but was awakened in the night by tremors and smoke. As the house's foundation began to crumble, they escaped on foot, holding pillows over their heads to protect from falling debris. But the air was thick with volcanic ash and gas, and the men likely asphyxiated within minutes.

While Pliny did not survive his expedition, fortune *did* favor his legacy— and one could argue that was his greatest hope. Pliny's *Natural Histories* remains a treasured resource, even informing the organization of modern encyclopedias.

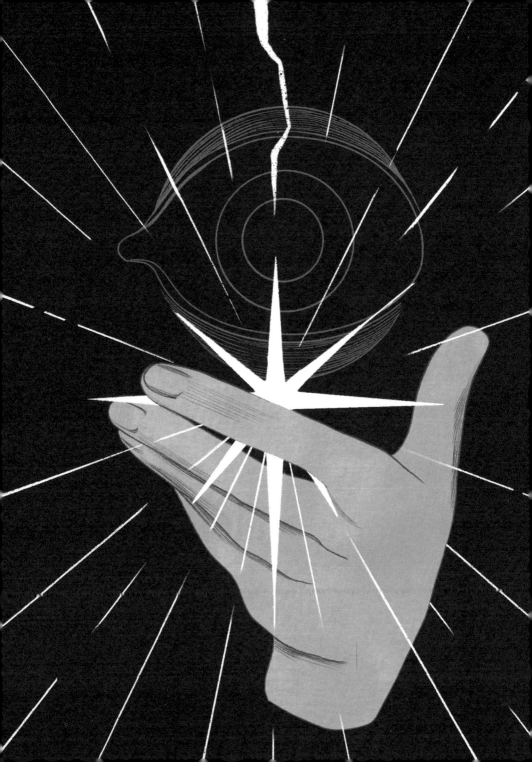

CARPE DIEM

MEANING: Seize the day
ATTRIBUTION: Horace
ORIGIN: *Odes* 1.11

In a short poem addressed to a female companion, Horace urges her not to ask "which end / the gods have given (her)" but instead to "wise up" and concern herself only with the present. The poem expresses an essentially Epicurean view of divinity and fate: The gods will not interfere in mortal matters, so don't waste time inquiring about their plans. While you do, time will continue to pass, and you will have missed the opportunity to truly live. *Carpe diem*, Horace writes—"seize the day"—*quam minimum credula postero*—"put very little trust in the next one."

Though this phrase is often quoted, its meaning has shifted over time. The Latin *carpe* means "to pluck," as in to harvest a ripened fruit, implying that the key to living well was not so much enthusiasm as timeliness. Similarly, Epicureanism is often mistaken for hedonism—the relentless pursuit of pleasure. While the Epicureans did value pleasure as the highest good, they—like their rivals, the Stoics—believed in restraint. Moderate pleasure was the key to a blessed life.

While similar in meaning to the Stoic phrase *memento mori*, the Epicurean *carpe diem* was oriented differently. Both phrases locate meaning in the present, but "memento mori" does so by invoking both past and future—*Remember*, you *will* die. By contrast, Horace's poem specifically counsels against imagining the future. The space in which meaning unfolds is here and now.

Nunc est bibendum

MEANING: Now is for drinking

ATTRIBUTION: Horace

ORIGIN: *Odes* 1.37.1

In his poem commemorating Cleopatra's death, Horace describes the queen as a fierce woman who died deliberately, calmly, and unafraid of the sword that came for her. He raises a toast—"Now is for drinking"—both in celebration of Cleopatra's downfall and in honor of her fearless leadership.

Revered and reviled, Queen Cleopatra of Egypt polarized Roman politics. Her suicide marked the end of Ptolemaic Egypt and the start of the country's Roman occupation. Marc Antony and Octavian had waged civil war, competing to succeed the late Julius Caesar. When Cleopatra's lover and ally, Marc Antony, lost to Octavian at the Battle of Actium in 31 BCE, the queen knew her days were numbered. In Horace's telling, rather than submit to what she saw as Octavian's arrogance, Cleopatra "welcomed a snake's venom," robbing her foe of his conquest.

Although Octavian may have hunted the doomed queen "like a hawk after a dove," in reality, Cleopatra's death did not immediately follow Marc Antony's defeat; her suicide occurred almost a year later. Horace snubs the facts in favor of a more dramatic story—and one that upheld Roman gender roles. In the poem's opening, he pictures Cleopatra stumbling, drunk with power, but in its final lines, she is sobered, sacrificing herself in traditional Roman fashion. "No low-born dame," in death, she becomes the ideal woman: subservient to the imperial agenda.

Similar to *carpe diem*, Horace's *nunc est bibendum* encourages the timely pursuit of pleasure: drink *now*, he urges—for none of us can know which sip will be our last.

SOL OMNIBUS LUCET

MEANING: The sun shines for everyone
ATTRIBUTION: Petronius
ORIGIN: *Satyricon* 100

"The sun shines for everyone"—even the enslaved. While this line from Petronius's novel the *Satyricon* may seem to express an egalitarian view, it was, in fact, a parody of Seneca the Younger's anti-slavery position. Petronius served as Emperor Nero's *arbiter elegantiarum*, or judge of elegance. Because his opinions on arts and culture became law, it was important that his sensibilities align with Nero's politics.

Petronius's line references one from Seneca the Younger's *Letters*—"I owe much to the sun and moon, yet they do not rise only for me"—but mocks its philosophy by placing it in a ridiculous context. Seneca argues, in Stoic fashion, that while anyone can become imprisoned by their desires, no person is naturally suited to enslavement. Liberty—like sunlight—is accessible by all. But in the *Satyricon*, Petronius writes of a rich man who is jealous that others covet his enslaved companion. Instead of peace and liberty, he suggests that attractive men belong to all: "I'm annoyed that the boy is pleasing to strangers," he says. "But aren't all of nature's best things made for communal enjoyment? The sun shines for everyone. The moon leads beasts to food . . ."

Roman slavery was a widespread institution: almost half of the population was either enslaved or formerly so. Many people were born into enslavement, which was passed down maternally, but others were enslaved as war captives, debtors, or criminals. In Rome, it was even legal to enslave an abandoned infant.

While Petronius did not struggle to align with Nero's views of slavery, he evidently disagreed with him on other issues. In 65 CE, Petronius was arrested for conspiring to overthrow the emperor. To avoid going to trial, Petronius killed himself—but not before ordering that his slaves receive a final set of lashes.

DEFICO
ILLEVS
VITAM
ET MENTEM
ET
MEMORIAM

Defico illeus vitam et mentem et memoriam

MEANING: I curse your life and mind and memory

ATTRIBUTION: Unknown

ORIGIN: *Roman Inscriptions of Britain* 7

This statement appears on a curse tablet recovered from Roman Londinium (modern London). Addressed to a woman called "Tretia Maria," it curses her organs to be mixed in her body and prays that she be unable to speak concealed things. Judging by its probable misspelling of "Tertia," the tablet may have been inscribed in haste, perhaps to address an urgent concern: its victim had acquired a precious secret.

Curse tablets, which evidenced a belief in ancient magic, were prolific in Rome. These were leaden tablets on which curses were inscribed. For the spell to go into effect, the tablets were buried in the yards of unsuspecting recipients. But there was a catch: By engraving a lead tablet, the curser inadvertently bound their life to the accursed, if not spiritually, then literally, in the form of lead poisoning. But there were ways of mitigating this consequence. Professional curse tablet authors inscribed personalized curses for a fee, and local magicians produced curse "templates," leaving blank spaces for the consumer to fill in. Rather cleverly, these same magicians also authored counter-curses and protective charms.

The popularity of curse tablets waned in the third century CE as Emperor Constantine began to police non-Christian religious customs—but one could argue that forms of the practice persist to this day. Romans' fears were not unique, nor was their lust for revenge.

FVGI
TENE
ME

FUGI, TENE ME

MEANING: I have fled, restrain me
ATTRIBUTION: Unknown
ORIGIN: Zoninus collar

In punishment for attempted escape, enslaved people in Rome were often forced to wear iron collars inscribed with this phrase. Physically and psychologically oppressive, the collars burdened their wearers both literally and in the form of humiliation.

Archaeologists have catalogued many items related to recaptured fugitives, including collars bearing other labels—"adulteress," for example. In every case, the intention was to insult the wearer and prevent them from fleeing. Commonly, these collars also bore the name of the enslaving family (or, in the case of the "adulteress," the name of her home region), ensuring that even far-flung fugitives would eventually be caught and returned.

This brutal practice was later adopted by American enslavers for many of the same purposes. American punishment collars were also made of iron and typically featured four lengthy prongs extending in each direction. These prongs would snag and catch on trees and bushes, making escape nearly impossible. They were also torture devices that prevented leaning, lying down, and sleeping.

In any slaveholding society, the prevalence of punishment collars suggests enslavers feared escape—or rebellion. In Rome, there were several slave revolts, referred to as the Servile Wars. In the third and final Servile War, the formerly enslaved gladiator Spartacus led more than 100,000 enslaved people into battle against the Roman legions. Ultimately, most of the enslaved people were killed; however, scholars suggest that the war began to disrupt traditional Roman perceptions of slavery. Over the course of the next few centuries, enslaved people won additional political rights—but never emancipation. Even so, these ancient uprisings would inspire later, more successful ones, including the Haitian Revolution of the 1790s and early 1800s, led by Toussaint Louverture, also known as "Black Spartacus."

PANEM ET CIRCENSES

MEANING: Bread and circuses
ATTRIBUTION: Juvenal
ORIGIN: *Satires* 4.10.81

W riting after the fall of the Roman Republic and without its protections, the satirist Juvenal relied on vague, witty language to convey his opinions. Of his fellow Romans, he famously quipped, "(they) desperately crave only two things: bread and circuses." Now a figure of speech meaning, essentially, superficial appeasements, *panem et circenses* was a veiled reference to certain policies and practices of Juvenal's day.

"Bread" may have referred to a series of reforms implemented by the Gracchi brothers, Tiberius and Gaius, in the second century BCE. The Gracchi were tribunes of the plebs who held exceptional power. At a time when Rome suffered severe poverty, Gaius Gracchi instituted the grain dole, which made several types of grain available to the lower classes. His brother, Tiberius, introduced land reforms that encouraged population growth and increased the number of people who were eligible to serve in the army.

"Circuses" called to mind the large entertainment complexes where Roman politicians sponsored public religious festivals and sporting events. These games, which included chariot racing, hunting, and parades, tended to coincide conspicuously with periods of economic recession or unrest.

Juvenal saw such reforms and amusements for what they were—mere "bread and circuses" intended to pacify the Roman people and distract them from their stripped political freedoms.

NEMO SALTAT SOBRIUS

MEANING: No one dances sober
ATTRIBUTION: Cicero
ORIGIN: *Pro Murena* 6.8

Accused of corruption and bribery, the former politician Lucius Licinius Murena hired the renowned lawyer Cicero to represent him in court. While the case concerned Murena's alleged fraud, Cicero defended his client by accusing the prosecutor, Cato, of slander: he had called Murena "a dancer."

In the Roman Republic, dancing was for entertainment purposes only. Dancers, like actors, were often lower-class or enslaved individuals who wore masks when they performed. "No one dances sober," Cicero explained, "unless he is insane." Therefore, Cato's accusation of vice amounted to defamation.

Ironically, Cicero would later be killed for writing a series of salacious speeches called the *Philippics*, in which he leveled scathing insults at Marc Antony. Not needing a court to seek justice, Marc Antony added Cicero's name to his proscription list—a hit list made public to Roman citizens—and disposed of Cicero rather neatly. According to the historian Plutarch, when Marc Antony's assassins caught up to Cicero, he bowed, exposing his neck in a gladiatorial display of surrender. By Marc Antony's order, Cicero's head and hands were nailed to the rostra, a podium in the Roman Forum.

In the end, it seems that Cicero's ethics were consistent: slander was unjust and intolerable. But—his actions suggest—sometimes a choice insult was worth losing one's head.

SUTOR, NE SUPRA CREPIDAM

MEANING: Shoemaker, not beyond the shoe
ATTRIBUTION: Pliny the Elder
ORIGIN: *Natural Histories* 35.36

In Pliny the Elder's *Natural Histories*, he tells the story of a shoemaker who, observing a painting by the Greek artist Apelles, notes that a sandal has too few straps. In response, Apelles amends the painting. Feeling encouraged, the shoemaker begins to point out *other* mistakes he thinks Apelles should fix. "Shoemaker, not beyond the shoe," the artist admonishes, implying that he should not offer advice beyond his own field of expertise.

This phrase, which Pliny notes became proverbial, is the source of the modern English term "ultracrepidarian"—someone in the habit of advising on matters they know nothing about—first penned by the British essayist William Hazlitt.

Despite Hazlitt's coinage, the saying might have passed into obscurity were it not for Karl Marx, who called it "sheer nonsense." Marx valued interdisciplinary work, citing technological advancements such as the steam engine (invented by a watchmaker) and the throstle (invented by a barber).

DAMNATIO MEMORIAE

MEANING: Damning of memory

ATTRIBUTION: Modern Latin to describe an ancient phenomenon

ORIGIN: C. Schreiter and J. H. Gerlach, *Dissertationem juridicam de damnatione memoriae: praescitu superiorum, in florentissima Philurea*

Memory was extremely important to the Romans. Living the *mos maiorum*, or the way of the ancestors, was the clearest path to personal and professional success. Historic greatness was acknowledged and monumentalized in the form of architecture, statuary, and poetry intended to outlast death. Therefore, *damnatio memoriae*—a punishment reserved for disgraced emperors—was the most damning fate imaginable. It virtually guaranteed that history would not remember you.

Due to its gravity, *damnatio memoriae* was not imposed casually; it involved a state-sponsored political process that was voted on by the Senate. Once decided, however, it was strictly enforced: the emperor was struck from historical records; inscriptions naming him were chiseled away; any statues commemorating him were defaced, their heads sometimes removed and replaced with those of other figures.

In actuality, the *complete* erasure of an emperor's historical record was difficult to achieve. For instance, the emperor Domitian—a paranoid autocrat who attempted to dissolve the Roman Senate—was both assassinated and condemned to oblivion. Except, of course, that he is remembered in these pages and others.

The true purpose of *damnatio memoriae*, therefore, may have been more abstract. According to Pliny the Elder, Romans took great pleasure in destroying statues of Domitian; it was a symbolic and visceral way of restoring justice. The process was also edifying for the Roman public. Not only did *damnatio memoriae* punish, it demonstrated, in no uncertain terms, that such behavior would not be tolerated.

But even the damning of memory was memorable. In place of the old monuments, there stood new ones: voids where the condemned once loomed, evidence of violence and loss.

Acknowledgments

Writing may be a solitary task, but books—like language—are collaborative. There are many people I'd like to thank for their contributions to this book:

Firstly, *Et Cetera* wouldn't exist without my wonderful collaborator, Marta Bertello, whose "Latin Phrases" series of illustrations inspired its concept. Of course, the book also would not exist without the amazing eye of our editor, Melissa Rhodes Zahorsky, or the wonderful advocacy of our agent, Alyssa Jennette. I'd also like to mention Marya Pasciuto, who delivered feedback I immediately trusted, and who withstood my constant grammatical quibbles. To the others on our editorial, design, and production team, including Brianna Westervelt, Diane Marsh, and Tamara Haus: Thank you for making this book a reality.

Thank you to Billy Collins, who kindly agreed to read my debut. I am so grateful for his endorsement, and for his generous gift to the Classics department at Holy Cross. With the help of his endowed scholarship, many more students will have access to a discipline that changed my life.

Additionally, I'd like to thank the many friends and advisers who supported my research. Thank you to Professors Lauren Capotosto,

Mary Ebbott, and Dominic Machado, who advised my thesis, "Classics in the Classroom," and under whose guidance I developed my pedagogical philosophies and a love of Classics that I hope is evident in this work. Thank you also to Professor Daniel Libatique, whose class "Roman Women and Men in Literature" remains one of the most impactful courses I've ever taken. (Readings from Professor Libatique's syllabus are peppered throughout my bibliography.) The biggest hugs to three high school teachers: Michael Mezzo, Amanda Telford (or, as I called her, Mag Telf), and Daniel Passarelli, who fostered an environment where I could be comfortably obsessed with the *Iliad*, or translation's inherent violence, or the Cuban Missile Crisis. Finally, thank you to the gracious few who scanned PDFs, borrowed library books, and accessed paywalled articles for me: Dr. Sneed, Sophia, Luke, Rose, Ellie, and Anne Catherine.

Of course, a book needs much more than an agent, editor, and collaborators to come into being. Thank you to Peter, Christine, James, Matthew & William, Christelle, Ruby, Mohamed, and Cydney, who offered their time and expertise, supported my personhood, or endured conversations in which I gestured wildly about "the narrative."

Bibliography

Andrade, Nathanael. "Voices in the Margins: Classics' Suppression of Ancient Roman Writers of Color." *Eidolon*, June 25, 2019. https://eidolon.pub/voices-in-the-margins-5f93acc0df6f.

Argetsinger, Kathryn. "Birthday Rituals: Friends and Patrons in Roman Poetry and Cult." *Classical Antiquity* 11, no. 2 (1992): 175–93. https://doi.org/10.2307/25010971.

Bartman, Elizabeth. "Hair and the Artifice of Roman Female Adornment." *American Journal of Archaeology* 105, no. 1 (2001): 1–25. https://doi.org/10.2307/507324.

Bond, Sarah. "The History of the Birthday and the Roman Calendar." *Forbes*, October 1, 2016. https://www.forbes.com/sites/drsarahbond/2016/10/01/the-history-of-the-birthday-and-the-roman-calendar/.

Caesar. *The Gallic War*. Translated by Jeffrey Edwards. Cambridge, MA: Harvard University Press, 1917. https://www.loebclassics.com/view/LCL072/1917/volume.xml.

Caesar, Julius. "The African Wars." Translated by W. A. McDevitte and W. S. Bohn. *The Internet Classics Archive*, n.d. http://classics.mit.edu/Caesar/african.html.

Catullus and Tibullus. *Catullus. Tibullus. Pervigilium Veneris*. Translated by F. W. Cornish. Cambridge, MA: Harvard University Press, 1913. https://www.loebclassics.com/view/LCL006/1913/volume.xml.

Cicero. *In Catilinam 1-4. Pro Murena. Pro Sulla. Pro Flacco.* Translated by C. Macdonald. Cambridge, MA: Harvard University Press, 1976. https://www.loebclassics.com/view/LCL324/1976/volume.xml.

Cixous, Hélène, and Catherine Clement. *The Newly Born Woman.* Translated by Betsy Wing. Minneapolis, MN: University of Minnesota Press, 1986.

Claassen, Jo-Marie. "Seizing the Zeitgeist: Ovid in Exile and Augustan Political Discourse." *Acta Classica* 59 (2016): 52–79.

Das, Nandini. "Time and Memory in Carthage." *Renaissance Studies* 35, no. 3 (2021): 360–85. https://doi.org/10.1111/rest.12705.

Fowler, W. Warde. "Passing under the Yoke." *The Classical Review* 27, no. 2 (1913): 48–51. https://www.jstor.org/stable/699756.

Gold, Barbara K. *A Companion to Roman Love Elegy.* Hoboken, NJ: John Wiley & Sons, 2012.

Gram, Lars Morten. "Odi et Amo: On Lesbia's Name in Catullus." In *Roman Receptions of Sappho*, edited by Thea S. Thorsen and Stephen Harrison. Oxford, UK: Oxford University Press, 2019. https://doi.org/10.1093/oso/9780198829430.003.0006.

Green, Steven J. "Malevolent Gods and Promethean Birds: Contesting Augury in Augustus's Rome." *Transactions of the American Philological Association (1974-)* 139, no. 1 (2009): 147–67. https://doi.org/10.1353/apa.0.0019.

Hairston, Eric Ashley. *The Ebony Column: Classics, Civilization, and the African American Reclamation of the West.* Knoxville, TN: University of Tennessee Press, 2013.

Harmon, Daniel P. *Religion in the Latin Elegists.* Berlin: Walter de Gruyter, 1986.

Hesiod. *Theogony. Works and Days. Testimonia.* Translated by Glenn W. Most. Cambridge, MA: Harvard University Press, 2018. https://www.loebclassics.com/view/LCL057/2018/volume.xml.

Homer. *Iliad.* Translated by Stanley Lombardo. Indianapolis, IN: Hackett Publishing Company, 1997.

Horace. *Odes and Epodes.* Translated by Niall Rudd. Cambridge, MA: Harvard University Press, 2004. https://www.loebclassics.com/view/LCL033/2004/volume.xml.

Joseph, Timothy. "The Verbs Make the Man: A Reading of Caesar, Gallic War 1.7 and Civil War 1.1 and 3.2." *New England Classical Journal* 44, no. 3 (2017): 150–61.

Judson, Anna P. "Women's Writing in the Ancient World." *It's All Greek To Me* (blog). March 6, 2020. https://itsallgreektoanna.wordpress.com/2020/03/06/womens-writing-in-the-ancient-world/.

Juvenal and Persius. *Juvenal and Persius.* Translated by Susanna Morton Braund. Cambridge, MA: Harvard University Press, 2004. https://www.loebclassics.com/view/LCL091/2004/volume.xml.

Kamen, Deborah. "Naturalized Desires and the Metamorphosis of Iphis." *Helios* 39, no. 1 (2012): 21–36. https://doi.org/10.1353/hel.2012.0000.

Kearsley, Rosalinde. "Octavian and Augury: The Years 30-27 B.C." *The Classical Quarterly* 59, no. 1 (2009): 147–66. https://www.jstor.org/stable/20616669.

Keith, Alison. "Critical Trends in Interpreting Sulpicia." *The Classical World* 100, no. 1 (2006): 3–10. https://doi.org/10.2307/25433969.

Laes, Christian, ed. *Disability in Antiquity.* London: Routledge, Taylor & Francis Group, 2017. https://doi.org/10.4324/9781315625287.

Lewis, A.-M. "Augustus and His Horoscope Reconsidered." *Phoenix* 62, no. 3/4 (2008): 308–37. https://www.jstor.org/stable/25651733.

Livy. *History of Rome, Volume IV.* Translated by B. O. Foster. Cambridge, MA: Harvard University Press, 1926. https://www.loebclassics.com/view/LCL191/1926/volume.xml.

Lucan. *The Civil War (Pharsalia)*. Translated by J. D. Duff. Cambridge, MA: Harvard University Press, 1928. https://www.loebclassics.com/view/LCL220/1928/volume.xml.

Mares, Martin. "Kleos, Nostos and Ponos in the Homeric Tradition." *The Classical Review* 67, no. 2 (2016): 64–71. https://papers.ssrn.com/abstract=3200025.

Martial. *Epigrams, Volume II*. Translated by D. R. Shackleton Bailey. Cambridge, MA: Harvard University Press, 1993. https://www.loebclassics.com/view/LCL095/1993/volume.xml.

Martin, Thomas R. *Ancient Rome: From Romulus to Justinian*. New Haven, CT: Yale University Press, 2012.

McCabe, Michael. "Hannibal Barca: For Carthage: The Right Man for the Wrong Time." *The Histories* 10, no. 1 (2019).

McGinn, Thomas A. J. "The Lex Lulia de Adulteriis Coercendis." In *Prostitution, Sexuality, and the Law in Ancient Rome*. New York: Oxford University Press, 2003. https://doi.org/10.1093/acprof:oso/9780195161328.003.0005.

Moore, Ken. "The Iphis Incident: Ovid's Accidental Discovery of Gender Dysphoria." *Athens Journal of History* 7, no. 2 (2021): 95–116. https://doi.org/10.30958/ajhis.7-2-1.

Morris, Ian, and Barry B. Powell, eds. *A New Companion to Homer*. Leiden, The Netherlands: Brill, 1997. https://brill.com/display/title/2264.

Morrison, Toni. "The Nobel Prize in Literature 1993." NobelPrize.org. https://www.nobelprize.org/prizes/literature/1993/morrison/lecture/.

Nayeri, Farah. "Rehabilitating Nero, an Emperor with a Bad Rap." *New York Times*, May 26, 2021. https://www.nytimes.com/2021/05/26/arts/design/nero-british-museum.html.

Ovid. *Heroides. Amores*. Translated by Grant Showerman. Cambridge, MA: Harvard University Press, 1914. https://www.loebclassics.com/view/LCL041/1914/volume.xml.

————. *Metamorphoses*. Translated by Stephanie McCarter. New York: Penguin Books, 2022.

————. *Tristia. Ex Ponto*. Translated by A. L. Wheeler. Cambridge, MA: Harvard University Press, 1924. https://www.loebclassics.com/view/LCL151/1924/volume.xml.

Pandey, Nandini. "Rome's 'Empire Without End' and the 'Endless' U.S. War on Terror." *Eidolon*, January 9, 2018. https://eidolon.pub/romes-empire-without-end-and-the-endless-u-s-war-on-terror-5c39ee3d0c66.

Petronius and Seneca. *Satyricon. Apocolocyntosis*. Translated by Gareth Schmeling. Cambridge, MA: Harvard University Press, 2020. https://www.loebclassics.com/view/LCL015/2020/volume.xml.

Plautus. *The Merchant. The Braggart Soldier. The Ghost. The Persian*. Translated by Wolfgang de Melo. Cambridge, MA: Harvard University Press, 2011. https://www.loebclassics.com/view/LCL163/2011/volume.xml.

Pliny. *Natural History, Volume IX: Books 33-35*. Translated by H. Rackham. Cambridge, MA: Harvard University Press, 1952. https://www.loebclassics.com/view/LCL394/1952/volume.xml.

————. *Natural History, Volume VIII: Books 28-32*. Translated by W. H. S. Jones. Cambridge, MA: Harvard University Press, 1963. https://www.loebclassics.com/view/LCL418/1963/volume.xml.

Quintilian. *The Orator's Education, Volume IV: Books 9-10*. Translated by Donald A. Russell. Cambridge, MA: Harvard University Press, 2002. https://www.loebclassics.com/view/LCL127/2002/volume.xml.

Redfern, Rebecca. "The Surprising Diversity of Roman London." *Museum of London*, July 1, 2018. https://www.museumoflondon.org.uk/discover/surprising-diversity-roman-london-docklands

Romano, David G. "Digital Augustan Rome." Accessed September 2, 2022. http://www.digitalaugustanrome.org/.

Rosengren, Amelie. "Cygnea Cantio: The Swan-Song." *Latinitium*,
September 13, 2017. https://latinitium.com/cygnea-cantio-the-
swan-song/.

Sappho. *If Not, Winter: Fragments of Sappho*. Translated by Anne Carson.
New York: Knopf Doubleday Publishing Group, 2003.

Segal, Charles. "Myth and Philosophy in the Metamorphoses: Ovid's
Augustanism and the Augustan Conclusion of Book XV." *The
American Journal of Philology* 90, no. 3 (1969): 257–92. https://doi.
org/10.2307/293179.

Sifuentes, Jesse. "Authority in Ancient Rome: Auctoritas, Potestas,
Imperium, and the Paterfamilias." *World History Encyclopedia*,
November 5, 2019. https://www.worldhistory.org/article/1472/authority-
in-ancient-rome-auctoritas-potestas-impe/.

Smith, R. Scott, and Christopher Francese, eds. *Ancient Rome: An Anthology
of Sources*. Indianapolis, IN: Hackett Publishing Company, Inc., 2014.

Starks, John H., Jr. "Fides Aeneia: The Transference of Punic Stereotypes
in the Aeneid." *The Classical Journal* 94, no. 3 (1999): 255–83. https://
www.jstor.org/stable/3298369.

Statius. *Thebaid, Volume I: Thebaid*. Translated by D. R. Shackleton
Bailey. Cambridge, MA: Harvard University Press, 2004. https://www.
loebclassics.com/view/LCL207/2004/volume.xml.

Suetonius. *Lives of the Caesars, Volume I*. Translated by J. C. Rolfe.
Cambridge, MA: Harvard University Press, 1914. https://www.
loebclassics.com/view/LCL031/1914/volume.xml.

Sulpicia. *Six Poems*. Translated by Anne Mahoney. Medford, MA: Perseus
Digital Library, 2000.

Tacitus. *Histories*. Translated by Clifford H. Moore. Cambridge, MA:
Harvard University Press, 1925. https://www.loebclassics.com/view/
LCL111/1925/volume.xml.

Tatum, W. Jeffrey. *Always I Am Caesar*. Malden, MA/Oxford: Blackwell Publishing, 2008.

Teets, Sarah. "Classical Slavery and Jeffersonian Racism." *Eidolon*, August 10, 2018. https://eidolon.pub/classical-slavery-and-jeffersonian-racism-28cbcdf53364

Terence. *Phormio. The Mother-in-Law. The Brothers*. Translated by John Barsby. Cambridge, MA: Harvard University Press, 2001. https://www.loebclassics.com/view/LCL023/2001/volume.xml

"Third Punic War: Carthage and Rome [149 BCE–146 BCE]." *Britannica*, June 10, 2023. https://www.britannica.com/event/Third-Punic-War.

Vergil. *Aeneid*. Translated by Shadi Bartsch. New York: Random House Publishing Group, 2021.

———. *Eclogues. Georgics. Aeneid: Books 1-6*. Translated by H. Rushton Fairclough. Cambridge, MA: Harvard University Press, 1916. https://www.loebclassics.com/view/LCL063/1916/volume.xml.

Walcott, Derek. *Omeros*. New York: Farrar, Straus and Giroux, 1992.

Washington, Booker T. *The Negro Problem: A Series of Articles by Representative American Negroes of Today*. New York: J. Pott & Co., 1903.

Weil, Simone. *Simone Weil's The Iliad or The Poem of Force: A Critical Edition*. Translated by James P. Holoka. New York: Peter Lang, 2003.

White, Peter. "Julius Caesar in Augustan Rome." *Phoenix* 42, no. 4 (1988): 334–56. https://doi.org/10.2307/1088658.

INDEX

Eos, xvii
epic poetry, 11, 17, 27, 79
Epictetus, 89
Epicureans, 55
    carpe diem and, 93
Epigrams (Martial), 40–41
Epistulae (Pliny the Elder
    via Pliny the Younger),
    90–91
*equo ne credite, timeo
    danaos et dona ferentes*
    (Don't trust the horse
    . . . I fear the Greeks,
    even those bringing
    gifts), 56–57
Erasmus, 22–23
et ama quod femina debes
    (and love how a woman
    should), 34–35
Eternal Flame of Rome, 45
Even today, we believe our
    Vestal Virgins (*vestales
    nostras hodie credimus*),
    44–45
evil eye, 73
*exegi monumentum aere
    perennius* (I erected
    monuments lasting
    longer than bronze), 2–3
exile, 5, 33

F

faciam ut mei memineris
    (I will force you to
    remember me), 18–19
faithfulness (*fides*), 45, 55
fascinum (phallic talisman),
    73
fate, 59, 71, 75, 85, 93, 109
father, 35, 37, 53, 71, 81
female leader (*dux femina*),
    31
fides (faithfulness), 45, 55
Field of Mars (*Campus
    Martius*), 77
fire, 11, 79

First, they were thrown in
    the river, then on top of
    bodies (*in fluvium primi
    cecidere, in corpora
    summi*), 78–79
foedus (polluted or foul),
    77
fortes fortuna iuvat
    (Fortune favors the
    brave), 90–91
friendship, xiv, 25–45
fugi, tene me (I am fleeing,
    restrain me), 100–101
funeral, 23, 39, 45

G

Gaius Gracchi, 103
Gallus, 27
gender roles, xiv, 35, 95
Georgics (Vergil), 9
Gerlach, J. H., 108–9
Gilgamesh, 35
golden mean poem, 55
Greece. *See specific topics*

H

Haitian Revolution, 101
Hannibal Barca, 84–85
Hazlitt, William, 107
Herculaneum, 91
Hercules, 51
Herodotus, 17
Heroides (Heroines)
    (Ovid), 58–59
Hesiod, 11
    Manilius and, 13
*hic vitam tribuit sed hic
    amicum* ([My birthday]
    gave me my life, but
    yours, a friend), 40–41
Homer, 17. *See also Iliad*
    Manilius and, 13
    Odyssey by, 9
homosexuality, 32–35, 43
Horace. *See Odes*

I

I am fleeing, restrain me
    (*fugi, tene me*), 100–101
I am holding a wolf by
    the ears (*auribus teneo
    lupum*), 20–21
I am holding you, Africa
    (*teneo te Africa*), 66–67
I curse your life and mind
    and memory (*defico
    illeus vitam et mentem et
    memoriam*), 98–99
I erected monuments
    lasting longer
    than bronze (*exegi
    monumentum aere
    perennius*), 2–3
I hate, and I love (*odi et
    amo*), 42–43
I will force you to
    remember me (*faciam ut
    mei memineris*), 18–19
Ianthe, 35
*igitur censuit Asinius
    Gallus ut libri Sibyllini
    adirentur* (Thus, Asinius
    Gallus suggested that
    the Sibylline Books be
    consulted), 60–61
Iliad (Homer), 9
    the Muses and, 11
    on swans, 23
immortal legacy (*kleos*),
    3, 9
imperium sine fine (Power
    without end), 70–71
*in fluvium primi cecidere,
    in corpora summi* (First,
    they were thrown in
    the river, then on top of
    bodies), 78–79
inscriptions, xvi
Institutio Oratoria
    (Quintilian), 16–17
invidia (envy), 73
invisus natalis adest (My
    annoying birthday is
    here), 36–37

About the Author
and Illustrator

Photo by George Annan

Maia Lee-Chin is a lover of casual conversations with the ancient world and is convinced that all translations are autobiographical. She claims she was born to be a classicist, citing her Greek goddess namesake and her lineage, which includes some of the earliest African Americans to obtain college degrees. When not writing, Maia plays video games, cooks, cleans (begrudgingly), works in urban education, and tries not to use epic poetry as a road map for life. She has other work featured in *Eidolon* and *Ancient Exchanges.*

Photo by Glorija Blazinšek

Marta Bertello grew up in Turin, Italy, where she graduated with honors from the Albertina Fine Art Academy. Her work focuses on suspended, slightly unsettling atmospheres, with special attention given to composition and visual storytelling. She lives and works in Venice.